SLOW BURN

D0503352

SLOW BURN
A Photodocument of Centralia, Pennsylvania

Photographs and Text by
Renée Jacobs

Introduction by
Margaret O. Kirk

UNIVERSITY OF PENNSYLVANIA PRESS
Philadelphia

Parts of this book have previously appeared in
the *Philadelphia Inquirer Magazine* and the *Boston Phoenix*.

Library of Congress Cataloging-in-Publication Data

Jacobs, Renée.
  Slow burn, a photodocument of Centralia, Pennsylvania.

  1. Mine fires—Prevention and control. 2. Mine gases
—Pennsylvania—Centralia. 3. Coal mines and mining—
Pennsylvania—Centralia. 4. Centralia (Pa.)—History.
I. Title.
TN315.J33 1986   363.3′79   86-19212
ISBN 0-8122-1235-5 (alk. paper)

Man can hardly even recognize the
devils of his own creation.
ALBERT SCHWEITZER

Contents

Acknowledgments

THE PEOPLE WHO gave selflessly to this project were numerous, and without their love, strength, and support Centralia would have undoubtedly remained just a faded news clipping for me.

In Centralia many people opened their homes and their lives to me. This is their book and I can only hope that they understand the depth of my gratitude. Charlie and Mary "Treasy" Gasperetti, Joan and Lou Girolami, Trish Catizone, Catharene Jurgill, Colleen Russen, Dennis Wolfe, Tommy Larkin, and Flo and Todd Domboski were among many who were kind.

The support and encouragement of my mother, father, and sister were invaluable. Paul Yonchek's belief in this book and in me helped me through many a bleak and tired moment. Barbara Abrams was there at the inception of this project, contributed the maps, and unfailingly supported me. I am thankful she would not let me quit. Janet Kole gave generously of her time and legal advice. Steve Shaw's assistance with the editing was invaluable, as were the comments on the writing by Phil Gutis of the *New York Times*. I cannot adequately express my love and thanks to these people.

I also thank Joe Logan of the *Philadelphia Inquirer* for his assistance with certain elements of the text blocks. Robin Warshaw, Bernard Stehle and Burk Uzzle also provided helpful suggestions.

Ilford provided generous assistance with materials and I thank them.

RENÉE JACOBS

Introduction

A WHISTLE BLEW the day the fire started in Centralia.

It sounded long and shrill, a warning to the residents of this obscure Pennsylvania mining borough that something was wrong. The whistle rang out from the town's fire station and echoed back and forth across the valley and up and down the main street, Locust Avenue. The whistle sounded that spring day in May 1962 because someone had spotted flames flicking up out of the old mining pit, the one on the southeast side of town, just below Odd Fellows Cemetery.

For several years the pit had been used as a garbage dump. Now the trash was on fire. When they heard the whistle, volunteer firemen and borough workers rushed to the abandoned mining pit, where they quickly shoveled clay and hosed water onto the flames to extinguish the fire. Before long, the flames were gone. The men turned and headed back to town.

What no one knew that day in Centralia, though, was that the fire still burned. It had simply dropped out of sight. As the men returned to their work, the smoldering fire was already spreading to a coal seam that lay in the ground below the open pit, a black river of coal that would gradually lead the fire into a massive honeycomb of underground mine tunnels, tunnels deep and thick and rich in anthracite coal that criss-crossed under the streets of Centralia.

And as the tunnels flowed, so spread the fire.

It took years, decades in fact, for the people of Centralia to realize that the ominous whistle blast they heard that spring day had anything to do with the dramatic changes in their lives. It was years later that the government placed ticking, black boxes in Centralia homes to monitor the carbon monoxide escaping from the underground fire. Years later that a twelve-year-old boy fell into a hole of three-hundred-degree heat that opened up before him on Valentine's

Day in the backyard of his grandmother's home. Years later that the members of the local chapter of the International Ladies Garment Workers' Union unfurled an American flag in the St. Ignatius Roman Catholic Church and sang proudly: "This town is your town / This town is my town / Don't let Cen-tral-i-a / burn forever."

Indeed, the whistle that one day pierced the lives of some one thousand Centralia residents has never been silenced. The fire that simply dropped out of sight twenty-four years ago still burns. No one knows how to put it out.

And this fire, this slow-burning fire, killed Centralia, Pennsylvania.

EVERYWHERE, YOU HEARD IT: "Centralia was a nice little town."

Before the fire, Centralia was a town where people lived out their lives content to marry, raise children, go to church, fix up grandma's house, and grow old, just like their ancestors who first settled into this northern bend of the Appalachian Mountains in 1855 and incorporated Centralia Borough in February 1866. As sure as the sun rose every morning, John Coddington sold gas at his Amoco station. Helen Womer worked as cashier at the local bank. The nearest movie theater was seventeen miles away, but no matter. Every July 4, just down the hill in the little patch town of Byrnesville, there would be a bonfire so big it could be seen from miles away. The Jurgills coached the Centralia Little League softball team every summer, and a body could get a beer and a shot for fifty-five cents down at Mekosh's on a Saturday night. Gossip would "travel up one end of the street and go back down the other side," Colleen Russen once said with affection for Centralia, where portraits of Jesus, John and Robert Kennedy, and the family's first bride hung on household walls.

How people loved to look out their windows and into their backyards, covered as they were with huckleberry bushes and mountain laurel. It was beautiful; but more importantly, it was theirs. In Centralia you could own your own home, walk to church in the morning, and pass the evening sitting on the front porch.

A sense of trust, a singular, blind trust, bound these Centralians together like a rich tapestry laid out on a mountaintop. It was the kind of trust that evolves from generations of loving and living and dying in the clusters of white, clapboard rowhouses that lined Locust Avenue and ran smack through the middle of town. It was the kind of trust based on that which is familiar. That which is predictable. And that which is fiercely proud.

The fire took all of this away. As the years passed and the fire continued to spread, the people of Centralia began to understand the true meaning of the whistle's warning. The tapestry of their town and their lives started to unravel, first one thread, then another.

Of paramount concern was something the Centralians had never thought to question. Were they safe in their own homes and their own backyards?

As the fire burned beneath the town streets and surrounding hills, the people started to worry. They had to beg before government officials offered to put black monitoring devices in their homes, devices that went "tick, tick, tick" in the corner, measuring the carbon monoxide gases that many thought were seeping in from the fire. If the gas reached too high a level, the boxes screamed. Eventually representatives from the state Department of Environmental Resources visited the homes to check for the presence of other toxic fumes. "Those boys from DER," as they were called, would often stop, chat, and have a cup of coffee with the neighbors, so expected was their knock at the front door.

Other visible reasons for concern surfaced. Because they lived in a mining town, Centralia residents were used to subsidences, those holes in the ground caused by loose soil giving way unexpectedly. But after the fire started, the subsidences were worse than ever before. Signs that read "Keep Out, Danger" were posted in backyards and empty lots where it was too dangerous for children to play. Some say the town was never quite the same after Todd Domboski survived a fall into a subsidence. The danger of the fire—heretofore played out in smoke on Route 61 and the ticking of the carbon monoxide monitors—became horribly real through the experience of this quiet, blond-headed child.

Many argued that health problems associated with carbon monoxide and the danger of the subsidences were highly exaggerated. But the sight of the boreholes would convince anyone that something was wrong in Centralia. The boreholes—those long, lean pipes sticking up out of the ground like freshly lit cigarettes with smoke rising from their tips—were used to vent the steam and smoke from the burning underground fire. There were at least eighteen hundred boreholes all over town; the ones closest to the old mining pit, where the fire started, were surrounded with material that looked like chicken wire. They were eerie, those boreholes. Their very silhouettes represented a ubiquitous, silent enemy that threatened to destroy the town.

Other threads in the town's tapestry, unrelated to the health and safety of its citizens, unraveled, too. Particularly when it came to the town's sense of community. That black river of coal running beneath Centralia, coal that was first mined here in 1842 and the very reason the town was ever born, had turned against the people. The town was literally divided into hot and cold sides, depending on whether a family lived on land directly above the tunnels of fire or above tunnels the fire had not yet reached.

As strange as it might seem, the citizens of Centralia could never agree on where the fire was located. Sometimes they could not even agree on whether there was a fire. After all, the fire is largely out of sight, except up at Big Mine Run, a mining pit on the southeast side of town where flames sometimes surface. Even without the flames, the smoke from the underground fire is particularly dense on cold or rainy days, when it settles above the pit like a heavy veil on a favorite straw hat. The smoky veil begs for an answer to an age-old question that so many take for granted: Where there is smoke, isn't there fire? In Centralia, answers to questions did not always come easy.

Even people living on the same side of town, in the impact zone where the fire was burning hotter than anywhere else, could not agree on what was happening under their own backyards. Some said that their basements were so warm from the nearby underground fire that they did not even need to turn on hot water heaters to heat the bath water; others would not even have monitors installed in their homes, so gas- and vapor-free did they trust them to be.

Some just did not care to know what was going on. It was all so complicated, so foreign, this notion of a fire underground, of vapors seeping into your home. Centralia, after all, was supposed to be "such a nice little town." So was it radon or radium, Mary Gallagher wanted to know, that was being measured in her basement by "that thing that looked like a ball of scotch tape?"

The tension became so great that it followed the residents into the most unlikely arenas of confrontation: their churches. Parishioners were often at odds with their priests. Mary Gasperetti, a devout Catholic, pulled her son out of the communion line one Easter Sunday before he received the sacrament from a priest who opposed her efforts to get out of town. On another occasion a priest requested that those leaving town donate their shrubbery to help make Centralia prettier for those who chose to stay. With that, a woman sitting in the congregation stood up and allowed that her rhododendron bushes were sixteen feet tall and very expensive and that she would be "a son of a bitch" before leaving them behind.

The fire without flames took its toll inside the borough's white, clapboard homes, too. The town's first mental health clinic opened. And many families, those who at first glance appeared as strong as the tapestry that once defined their community, learned the meaning of true stress.

Catharene Jurgill, for one, had married her high school sweetheart, started her family, and taken care of her home, never dreaming that something like a mine fire would disrupt her life. But when the fire spread and she became active in the movement to get out of Centralia, her marriage suffered. Eventually she and her husband separated, and she took their two daughters to live in another town.

Flo Domboski, who had invested all her money in her house and planned to live there forever, had never thought of a life anywhere but in Centralia. Then, on Valentine's Day in 1981, her son, Todd, fell into a hole in the backyard of his grandmother's house. When the earth gave way under his feet, there was only the smell of sulfur, the smoke, the terribly hot temperature. As he fell, he grabbed onto some tree roots sticking out of the loose earth and reached up for his cousin's hand. To this day, people say that Todd Domboski should not be alive. His mother decided to take no more chances. No house was more important than her son's safety. The Domboskis moved away.

Joan Girolami became an activist. She and a handful of other residents formed a group called Concerned Citizens Against the Mine Fire, which demanded that the government find a way to put out the fire. The former homemaker and mother of two, her head so full of hot-curled blond hair that they used to call her "Joanie Fawcett," lobbied in Washington, D.C., gave interviews on national television, talked to the press, and watched as the klieg lights of a documentary film crew burned her kitchen ceiling. Many people in town turned against her: She represented too much change, too much that was unpredictable and out of control in their little town.

"You know, they say small towns are so nice," Joan Girolami once said. "Put a tragedy in a small town, you'll find out how nice it is. Put a disaster there, and it's not so nice anymore."

Two months after the whistle sounded its warning, town officials met with experts from the Pennsylvania Department of Mines and Mineral Industries to discuss the fire. For the next twenty-four years, the people of Centralia believed that the state and federal governments would put out the fire and keep their town safe. And the government officials did try. They excavated burning material and made plans to construct an underground barrier to stop the fire; on more than one occasion, the fire burned and moved so quickly that the barrier became useless even before it was built. Underground tunnels were pumped full of fly ash to try and stop the fire from spreading. Clay seals were placed in the excavation areas to cut oxygen off from the fire. Nothing worked.

And so the houses started to come down.

On May 22, 1969, the government moved three families from the corner of Wood and South Streets, an area in the impact zone. The fire was cutting off the oxygen in these homes; traces of carbon monoxide and high temperature made them virtual time bombs. No state or federal authority had yet to declare the town of Centralia a disaster area, but these three homes were the first to be considered unsafe. They would not be the last.

It is important to remember that nearly two decades passed before the people of Centralia understood that the government and all its efforts to stop the fire might not keep them safe. Until the late 1970s, there was never the sense that the government might fail or that the fire was burning out of control. Truth to tell, that is exactly what happened.

From 1962 to 1984 federal and state officials from the Department of Environmental Resources, the Office of Surface Mining, and the Bureau of Mines in the U.S. Department of the Interior spent more than seven million dollars trying to put the fire out. Official reports on the state of the fire, however, were never encouraging. On the contrary, the reports seemed always to conclude that the blaze was getting worse. At one point the fire burned nearly three hundred feet below the surface and registered temperatures of over seven hundred degrees. Among Centralians there were reports that vegetables growing in backyard gardens had burned to a crisp.

In 1980 the U.S. Bureau of Mines released a thick, sobering report that devastated the citizens of Centralia. Called the "Red Book" for the color of its cover, the report made clear what the whistle had first tried to warn: "The Centralia mine fire has not been extinguished and is not controlled. The measures used to date in attempts to control the fire have not been effective and in some cases may have influenced the propagation of the fire."

The same year the Red Book was released, twenty-seven families sold their homes to the federal government. Many of them sold their homes for virtually nothing, not caring to wait for any regulated buy-out program that would have given them more money. They simply wanted out. Centralia was no longer such a nice, little town. Indeed, the Centralians had completely lost faith in that blanket of protection called government. There was even talk of a conspiracy existing between the coal companies and government officials, a conspiracy to get the people out of Centralia so the companies could mine the valuable coal assets underneath the town. Why shouldn't that explain what was going on? the people asked. The coal, after all, was rumored to be worth more than fifteen million dollars.

The bitterness felt by the residents toward the government surfaced openly in their own ranks. In late 1979 the Concerned Citizens group was formed by Girolami. At first it tried to pressure the government to find a way to put out the fire. When that proved futile, the group became known as the Centralia Committee for Human Development. This committee was dedicated to getting money for the families who wanted to sell their homes and move elsewhere.

Before long, an opposition group called Residents to Save the Borough of Centralia was formed, dedicated to preserving the community at all costs. The group's members were convinced that if a fire was burning under the town—and they were not at all convinced that there was—it was not really that bad.

The conflict between the groups was intense. In fact, when Helen Womer, a leader in Residents to Save the Borough of Centralia, and Girolami were scheduled to appear on the same television talk show, they refused to ride to the studio in the same limousine.

In 1983 yet another report stated that the mine fire was now burning on not one but on three or four fronts. Moreover, it was reported that the fire had the potential to damage nearly thirty-seven hundred acres encompassing Centralia and several small neighboring towns. On August 11, 1983, the residents of Centralia voted overwhelmingly (345 to 200) to take advantage of a voluntary federal government buy-out program that would allow them and the eighty residents of neighboring Byrnesville to sell their homes and move away from the fire. Three months later the federal government voted to appropriate forty-two million dollars in funds for the program.

After twenty-four years the government finally told the people of Centralia that their homes were not safe. That the fire was causing problems that could never be repaired. That the fire was burning out of control. And that the people here had a right to start a new life, somewhere else.

One by one, blood-red numbers were painted on the houses that had been sold and marked for demolition. On December 14, 1984, the bulldozers started tearing them down.

ONCE, WHEN YOU STOOD at the crest of Aristes Highway and gazed at the rows of white, clapboard houses, Centralia looked like an average town, a sort of toy town of paved streets, church steeples, and patches of grass in backyards. Today, many of the blocks are missing. The toy town has fewer and fewer houses. The steeples are gone. And the patches of grass no longer represent only backyards. Grass has been planted where houses once stood.

In 1985 alone approximately one hundred homes were torn down. The voluntary government buy-out program will be available to Centralia's residents until the end of 1986. After that, common wisdom goes, there will be few, if any, families left living in Centralia.

Helen Womer is one who has opted not to leave Centralia. When the government buy-out program is finished, she said, those left in Centralia "will be the most close-knit, dedicated group of people you will ever hope to meet." When the United Methodist Church was torn down on August 20, 1985, Mrs. Womer watched, taking pictures with her camera. Before the steeple was ripped off, she clicked and then turned to leave. "Sick, sick," she muttered to herself.

The ones who chose to leave are scattered, some to houses in neighboring communities, others to little-known towns clear across the country. Some have chosen to be a part of Den-Mar Gardens, a community of homes being built about seven miles from Centralia on land purchased with so-called "last resort money" from the federal government. The Centralia Homeowners Association, an offshoot of the original Concerned Citizens group, coordinated the new community.

Den-Mar Gardens has lots for more than one hundred new homes and apartments, as well as plans for a community center and some shops. In the Centralia Homeowners Association office, a map sprinkled with little red dots allows that dozens of residents will be a part of this new community. The project is being coordinated by Sister Honor Murphy, who was assigned to Centralia in 1983 and has worked in disaster relief service since the early 1970s. A Mother Jones poster on the wall of her office tells the story of her life, her creed: Pray for the Dead, Fight like Hell for the Living.

And there is no doubt, though, that even Sister Honor cannot put Centralia together again. The tapestry that was once Centralia is all but gone now, frayed to the point that it no longer exists. After twenty-four years of living with the fire that burns beneath their town, the people of Centralia have heeded the whistle's warning.

They have no doubt wondered, time and again, about the decades-old story often repeated in Centralia, the one about the priest and the roving labor gang called the Molly Maguires. Legend has it that the priest once denounced the Mollys from his pulpit. Later, as he prayed in the cemetery, the angry Mollys returned and beat him. The priest managed to stagger back to the church, where he summoned all his parishioners by ringing the church bell. When they arrived, he told them this: From that day forth, there would be a curse on the town of Centralia.

The little mountain mining town, founded on a bed of coal, would burn forever.

Maps

Previous government fire abatement measures, 1962–1973

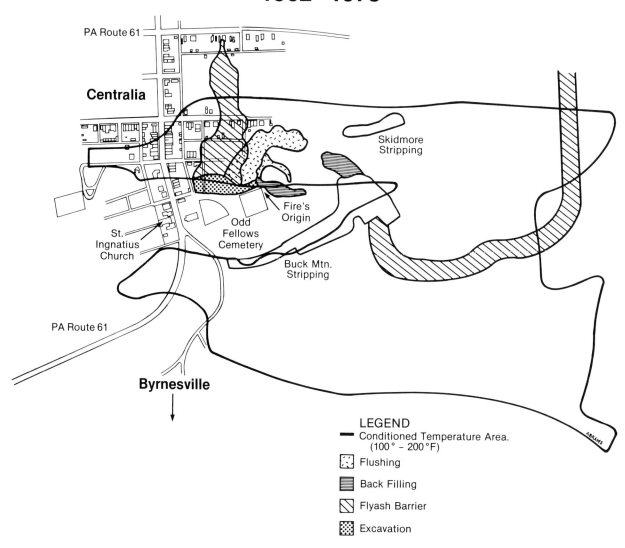

PA Route 61

Centralia

Skidmore
Stripping

Fire's
Origin

St.
Ingnatius
Church

Odd
Fellows
Cemetery

Buck Mtn.
Stripping

PA Route 61

Byrnesville

LEGEND
— Conditioned Temperature Area.
(100° – 200°F)
Flushing
Back Filling
Flyash Barrier
Excavation

Potential trenches for fire containment, 1983
(approximate total cost—$103.5 million)

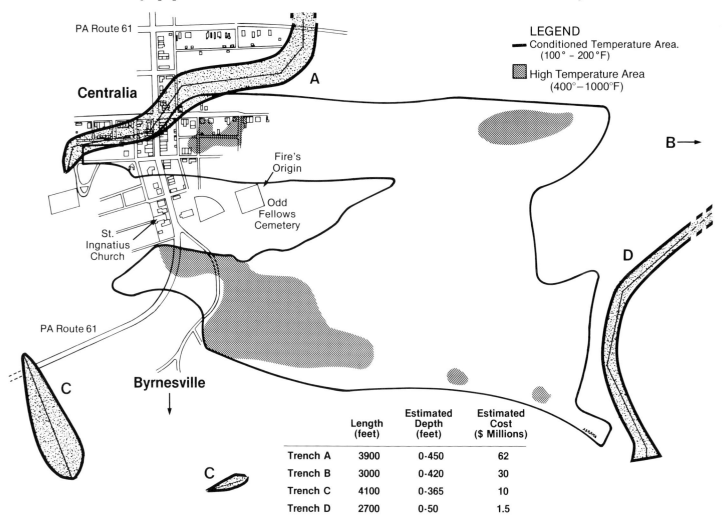

LEGEND
— Conditioned Temperature Area.
(100° – 200°F)

High Temperature Area
(400°–1000°F)

PA Route 61

Centralia

A

B→

Fire's
Origin

Odd
Fellows
Cemetery

St.
Ingnatius
Church

D

PA Route 61

Byrnesville

C

C

	Length (feet)	Estimated Depth (feet)	Estimated Cost ($ Millions)
Trench A	3900	0-450	62
Trench B	3000	0-420	30
Trench C	4100	0-365	10
Trench D	2700	0-50	1.5

Centralia:
The Slow Burn

Smoke from the underground fire escapes through a vent, lessening the possibility of toxic gas buildup in nearby homes.

THE COAL COMPANY that used to own that land went out of business. It was an abandoned stripping when it all started. My God, it was terrible. There was supposed to be a trench to cut off the mine fire. They started digging it out here, past my backyard, went up one hundred fifty feet and quit. They quit for lack of funds, fifty thousand dollars short. That was 1969.

They had it out when they started digging the first time. All they needed was to dig another shift. They were only digging one shift a day. They should be digging three shifts a day when they're digging a mine fire. They always did before that, and since that, on every other mine fire job. What the hell. They had it out and it came to Labor Day. They had it dug right out, at the corner of the cemetery up here, and they laid off for five days. I went down in that pit and looked at it, and I could see the fire swirling this way.

Oh my God. It was beautiful back then. The huckleberries, yeah, Christ. We'd go back there; it was all huckleberry bushes and laurel bushes. That's all destroyed now. They destroyed this town, all right.

Well, hell. The whole town's dipping down in the middle there. The hill would get so steep, the cars couldn't get up in the middle. I don't think they're gonna do anything. They're gonna do what they did before. That's taking the homes. Instead of putting the fire out, they're gonna put the people out. I told the council in 1976 all about what's happening today. And the president of the council said to me, "If anybody would know about it, we would." And I said, "Well, I'm telling you." 'Cause I followed every borehole. I knew just how the fire was traveling. How the heat was traveling.

And they laughed at me.

ANTHONY GAUGHAN, 60,
retired coal miner. Born in Centralia, Gaughan worked all his life in the mines below the town. A lifelong resident of the impact zone, he died of black lung disease in January 1986.

Flo and Todd Domboski.

I FELL INTO the subsidence on February 14, 1981. I was twelve. My cousin and me were fixing a motorcycle near my grandmother's, and I saw a little smoke a couple of yards from where we were working on the bike. So I went over and brushed away some leaves 'cause I thought someone had thrown a match and I wanted to make sure there was no fire. And the ground just started giving way, and I went down to my knees, then my waist, and just kept going. I grabbed onto some roots and was screaming for my cousin. I couldn't see him; there was smoke everywhere. I just heard him screaming, "Put your hand up! Put your hand up!" I was in over my head when he finally grabbed me. It smelled like sulfur. It was unbearably hot, and it sounded like the wind howling down there.

TODD DOMBOSKI.

HIS GRANDMOTHER CALLED up and said, "Get over here. Todd fell in a hole with water or something and he's awfully dirty." So I went up through Apple Alley and saw all the smoke, and it started dawning on me and I sort of panicked. I went to hug him, grab him, and hold him, and he just sort of pushed me away and said, "I'm okay." There was a whole bunch of officials across the street looking at the fire, and one of 'em told me to take him up to the hosey for some oxygen and the mayor suggested I take him to the hospital for a blood-gas test. That night I was sitting down and it hit me. I could have lost him. I really could have lost him.

FLORENCE DOMBOSKI, *Todd's mother.*

I FELT REALLY lightheaded and like I was gonna pass out at the hospital. They couldn't believe I was alive and that I didn't have brain damage. The hole turned out to be close to three hundred feet deep, three hundred fifty degrees, and eleven hundred parts per million carbon monoxide. That night I couldn't sleep right, couldn't have anything over me like a blanket. Ever since, I've had terrible nightmares about falling in that hole.

TODD DOMBOSKI.

As SOON AS I got out of the hole, I knew it was God that saved me. Mom said she thinks He sent the Blessed Mother. I believe that my falling in the subsidence was to bring a point across to all of us. There was a reason. Like, "The fire's there. Don't ignore it." If it was a fire on the top of the ground and you could see it, you'd have to face it. You can't see it, so people don't face it. There are people in Centralia whose backyards are caving in and they're out there with shovels trying to fill it back in. I guess they'll just wait until someone gets killed to do something.

It's scary to think about Centralia, but it's scarier to think about nuclear power, nuclear weapons. That's just something that shouldn't be. They don't know how dangerous that stuff is. Plutonium and nuclear waste—that stuff lives twenty thousand years. It was a matter of seconds before total meltdown at Three Mile Island and that would have been thousands of lives. I'd just like to see what the government would have done if they had been in our position. Or the victims' at Three Mile Island. God, I'd really like to go to a place where there's no mine fire, no nuclear power plants. . . .

TODD DOMBOSKI.

TODD WOULD GO up the street to school, and I'd be petrified until he walked in the house. But what the devil was so safe about the house? The cellar was hot. I just wanted to move out after he fell in.

The state bought our house in the first relocation, but it was depreciated 20 percent for the mine fire. They didn't help at all with the move, so we moved by car since I couldn't afford a moving van. They took our whole row—boarded 'em up and knocked 'em down. It was horrible. I can never go home again. They robbed me of something I loved.

I don't know if it affected my health permanently. Just have to wait and see. I'm waiting to see about Todd. I don't care about myself. My life's half over, but his is just starting. I realized in my old block and on my mother's on Locust Avenue all these women had breast cancer, breasts removed. A lot died. I had a beautiful collie dog and a parakeet. They both died with cancerous tumors. When I put that all together, it was sheer panic.

FLO DOMBOSKI.

Department of Transportation officials survey a potential cave-in site off Route 61, the main road through Centralia.

WE DON'T HAVE a problem here. The kids play up and down the street. There's no gas here, no problem with the boreholes. But across the backyard where it outcrops to the surface and where Todd fell in—that's dangerous. If a kid falls in there, he's not getting out. I don't know how Todd did.

The hole wouldn't have to be very big to scald you to death either. They filled that one with a couple of wheelbarrows' worth of dirt. I'd sure feel guilty if anything happened to one of my kids. Wouldn't you?

But everyone has that little voice inside that tells them what's right and wrong, and if I leave I'll be going against what that voice tells me is right—my heritage, my past, and my soul.

JOSEPH SMOLOCK.

OUR CHILDREN LOVE it here. Bryan loves the digging and the trucks and all the machinery. We've tried to keep him away from too far past the backyard. At the same time, we don't want to put a fear into him.

Our strongest convictions as parents made us decide to stay. Centralia is a lovely town filled with so much heritage and beauty. There will always be a Centralia in our hearts and that sustains us. Whatever the future brings, we'll just have to survive.

SHARON SMOLOCK.

Bryan Smolock, 3, plays outside his backyard near a borehole, one of hundreds in
and around Centralia used to measure the
scope and temperature of the fire.

Holding her niece, Heather Hefner, 5, Mary McGinley stands in the Centralia Commit- *tee for Human Development office, waiting for news on the fire.*

WE WERE TOLD right out that the mine fire was dangerous to young kids because their lungs are more sensitive. When I babysit for my cousin, I don't take Heather up to the ball field anymore. The kids that live up there in the danger area have upper respiratory problems, and some of them look terrible. My God, if they were my kids, I would have said to hell with the house and moved. Some of those kids have watery eyes, and they're all white. No house is worth that.

Most people in Centralia have black lung and other lung diseases. I have asthma and it's real hard on me. I ended up in the hospital in intensive care with gas in my lungs. It took five days to get it out. My doctor told me that if I went up the hill past the Legion, he wouldn't take care of me anymore because of the gases at St. Ignatius. It was a sore spot in the family because Father Tony, the priest up there, is my husband's uncle. He told me not to use that as an excuse not to go to church. He thought that it was all in our minds, that there was no danger, and that we were selling out the town.

It got so bad that I was taking Librium for my nerves, too much Librium. It wasn't helping. It was those meetings that did it. You'd go to a meeting and they'd tell you one thing, next week something else. The Centralia Committee for Human Development was the only thing that helped with getting information. I learned the hard way you can never win against the government. I knew they were lying; you'd have to be blind not to see it. I went to one meeting with all the big shots from Harrisburg. A guy who worked in the mines with my father got up to try and explain the slopes in the mines, and this one big shot who was younger than me told him to sit down and shut up or they wouldn't do anything for Centralia.

MARY McGINLEY.

THE BYRNESVILLE BONFIRE'S been going on for more than one hundred years, from the beginning of the town. In 1983 we made a dummy of James Watt with the bald head and a sign that said, "Let it Burn, Jim," criticizing him for his lack of interest in the fire. When he was secretary of the interior and he was called in to help Centralia, he just said, "Let it burn," because it wasn't big enough to worry about. I guess our congressmen and our state reps approached him. It was really implanted in our minds what he had said, so we decided we were going to burn him that year. "Let it burn" is kind of final.

We'd start working on the bonfire late in May or early June, so by July 3 we'd have it really big. All the kids in Byrnesville would build it. We'd carry wood in our arms for hundreds of yards. You could feel Byrnesville getting really hepped up every year for it. When you'd walk down the street to go to work on it, neighbors would be out on their porches saying, "Oh, the bonfire looks really good this year." People would cut their grass and get all ready for it. We'd call the tire company in Ashland and have them bring up hundreds of tires. We used to have people camp out so kids from other towns wouldn't burn it down. You could see the flame for miles; it usually smoldered for three to four days, sometimes a week.

It was a great feeling to see James Watt burn. I wish he would have been here to watch.

TRISH CATIZONE, 21,
former president of Concerned Citizens.

At the annual July 4 Byrnesville bonfire, Jerry, 5, and Francine, 6, Anoia, stand in front of an effigy of former Secretary of the Interior James Watt, who once said that the federal government should not get involved in Centralia.

20

EVERY SO OFTEN the road would be closed. And we'd have to go down to Byrnesville to get in and out of town. There were a lot of wrecks, on account of the road, and you couldn't see because of the fumes. A little wind came, and it blew all the fumes down toward our places. People couldn't even see to drive. They had to stop and put their lights on, and put their heads out their windows to see the road and the yellow lines. That's the only way they could come through Centralia.

CLARA GALLAGHER.

*Route 61 was often closed when smoke and
fumes from the fire restricted visibility.*

Jack Chapman, 11 (far left), and members of the Centralia Youth Organization baseball *team on the steps of the Centralia Committee for Human Development office.*

IT NEVER BOTHERED us—playing up on the ball field with the vents. We always had a good baseball team. One girls' team wouldn't play our girls' team, though. They thought it was dangerous up there, so they canceled.

My friends and me would talk about the mine fire sometimes, but not a lot. We'd ride our motorcycles up by the vents and up by where Todd fell in. Up there I'd just ride faster and hope the ground wouldn't go. My folks told me to stay away, but we usually would play up there anyway.

The gases didn't really bother any of us. The people that were always around it got headaches, but none of my friends really.

The kids don't want to move and think the government should've done something twenty years ago to help us. So I don't think too much of them. I don't think they're going to do anything about the fire; maybe they'll try and put it out after they get the whole town out and start digging for coal.

I'd rather grow up here in Centralia. It's a small place and you know everybody. I don't like cities. If there were little kids here for my kids to grow up with, I'd want to raise them here when I have them. But only if the mine fire weren't here. 'Cause they could be out playing and one of those holes in the ground could open up. I was afraid that would happen to us while we were going up to church. I used to pray that it would all get cleared up and that there would be no more mine fire.

I'd stay if all the kids stay. But I don't want to be, you know, like the last kid in Centralia.

JACK CHAPMAN, 11,
a member of the Centralia Youth Organization baseball team.

I DIDN'T THINK the monitor was necessary, but they said it was. My monitor only went off once that I know of. Someone was supposed to know and come up and check it. But that morning it went off, nobody came.

I had just gone to bed. Turned the television off and I couldn't figure out what I was listening to. I had never heard it go off. But you'd think it was a big Mack truck out front. I came to the front and looked out, and it was a quarter of one in the morning and there was nothing out there. So I went to the cellar door and looked down, and that was where it was coming from. I thought, "There's some carbon monoxide down there, but it's not gonna bother me. If it's gonna take me, it's gonna take me." I sat up for almost two hours. I didn't do a darn thing. I had the windows open upstairs. I thought, "If I'm still here at three o'clock, I'm going to go to bed."

MARY DARRAH, 71.
Darrah has lived in her house in Centralia's impact zone since 1928. She would like to relocate to Beaver Creek, Ohio, to live with her son.

Rows of monitors used to test for carbon monoxide stored in the Department of Environmental Resources office.

I DON'T THINK there ever was a fire in the borough. It was in Conyngham Township. Behind the church it was six or seven hundred degrees, but now it's down and it's going east and west. If you go east about two miles down the mountain, you'll see it burning down there and the smoke; but I don't believe there are any gases in Centralia. They might dig a trench out there, and some say it's for the coal. But you talk to the miners who worked underneath the town, and some say there's hardly any coal there and others say there's billions of tons. I don't know who to believe.

I lived all my live here in Centralia, all sixty years. My homestead is here; I raised seven children here. My dad came over from Europe in the early 1920s, and he worked hard in the mines till he got miner's asthma. I thought about moving away once, but I changed my mind. Centralia's my home and I just want to stay.

I blame the state for letting the fire start. There was a borough dump on the west end of town. The state condemned it and then approved that hole in back of the cemetery on the east side of town as a dump. They started hauling garbage there and dumping it in. It had been an open pit where they had tried to get coal, but there weren't no coal and they were probably dumping there for a long time. It just accumulated for a number of years before the state approved of it as a dump.

I was up there the day the fire started. I had just finished two terms on borough council, and I guess I had it in my mind that I was still on it. When I heard the fire engines, I went up to see what was going on. You could see the garbage burning. It was just a small fire, but the fire trucks couldn't do anything so they got a bulldozer and that didn't do anything. The fire was down too far and the coal and the timber started to burn. God knows how deep the pit was. That's why they couldn't get water to the spot. I remember turning to the fire chief's wife and saying, "Betty, it'll take a long time to get this out now."

I was up on the corner the other day, and a car stopped and the guy said, "Boy, your town's getting dead." And I said, "Yeah, but it's sure laid out nice."

JERRY "SLAVY" WYSOCHANSKY.

Jerry "Slavy" Wysochansky.

SIX YEARS OF meetings, studies, surveys, engineering evaluations, borehole analyses, relocation projects, referendums, petitions, mind-manipulating tactics, exploitation by every conceivable source and still the root of the problem remains ignored. Since 1978 nothing has been done to prevent the effects of the mine fire from threatening our communities, a mind-boggling blatant violation of our right to life, liberty, and the pursuit of happiness.

We cannot help questioning the integrity of government agencies who consistently ignore these rights and allow this farce to continue.

Residents to Save the Borough of Centralia fact sheets.

On a winter night, with snow starting to fall and visibility dropping, signs have already been put into place to shut down Route 61.

Jeanine, 6, and Katrina, 3, Klementovich.

THE SAFETY OF my kids is my biggest concern, and the gas in the house terrifies me. I was happy to see the monitor put in. It used to go off a lot. I couldn't believe that people would say there were no gases in town.

It became very matter-of-fact for the kids, like second nature to them. Wayne and Dennis from DER [Department of Environmental Resources] would come to check for gases every day. They would let the kids watch the testing and explain to them what to do in case the monitor went off. They demystified it for them. The alarm itself would scare anybody, but most times it went off during the night and luckily they're very sound sleepers so it wouldn't wake them.

My sister and I didn't grow up worrying about the fire. In fact, when the fire first broke out, my sister and all the kids would go up and throw rocks in the pit. The fire was all the way down at the bottom. You could only see a tiny little bit of smoke if you caught it on the right day. I remember they dug down to it and turned it all over with dirt and said everything was all right. When they took the first houses in 1969, everybody thought that it was a fluke.

My father worked for a coal company, and in the 1960s he said they would have to strip it and it wasn't even a serious problem then. He predicted that we'd see Centralia gone.

Our homestead was a big white house right across from Coddington's gas station and right next door to where Todd fell in. My mother moved to Ashland in the relocation of 1981. She had been a lifelong resident. I've lived in Centralia all my life with the exception of two years. The kids were upset when they saw their grandmother's house bulldozed. There's a lot lost there that we could have had. But once that house was gone—as far as the sentiment for the town—that was it. Once that went, I wanted to get out of the town. I grew up in that house. I really thought we'd still be there. My father grew up in it. His father had built it. It was always in the family. I'm sure it was one of the first houses to be built in town.

I don't think I'll ever lose what I got from Centralia—the small town life and values. That's going to go with me no matter where I go. It's unfortunate that the kids won't be raised in Centralia. Hopefully what they get will be just as good.

The kids really don't understand enough to be afraid. I don't think the impact has fully hit the adults, let alone the kids.

SHEILA KLEMENTOVICH, 33.

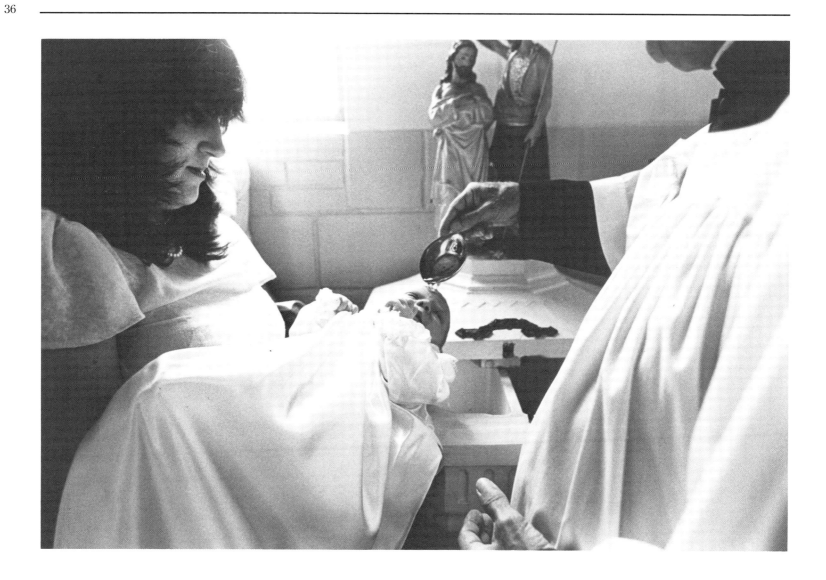

I DO BELIEVE that the fire is a sort of test of faith. The Lord does not necessarily send crosses but He permits crosses to come, and it's an occasion when people of faith have to believe that the Lord is near to them. I'm reminded of the gospel where the Lord seems to be asleep during a sudden storm, and when He was roused, He stilled the storm. Whenever there are storms in our lives of any kind, we have to believe that the Lord is near. He may seem to be sleeping, but He is near.

The Centralians are certainly bearing a difficult burden. Our priests, our bishops, the Holy Father, and all our people around the diocese, we're all pulling for them to make the right decisions and to persevere in them, whether it be to stay or go. I haven't got any crystal ball to see how things are going to play out. We support the presence of St. Ignatius. If anything, the people need the church more than ever. It's the center of their lives in these situations.

On December 3, 1983, as part of the five-year report that each bishop around the world must make to the Holy Father in Rome, I spent some time alone with Pope John Paul II. Before him, I placed a map of the diocese of Harrisburg with Centralia underlined. I told the Holy Father about the mine fire and the distress that this is causing the people. He listened with great attention and asked me to convey to the people of Centralia his affection and blessing.

THE MOST REVEREND WILLIAM KEELER,
Bishop of Harrisburg.

Elizabeth Gillespie (left) and her sister,
Kit Kane, in their Centralia home.

THE MINE FIRE is disgusting. I don't like to think of it. It ruined Centralia. We had a beautiful church, school, and convent. They tell me that has to go. I never thought we would have to go. I thought I'd still be here when I died, but they fooled me.

They said the fire was starting to come into Centralia, but I don't know anything about the mines. Everytime you'd talk to somebody, they'd say, "Oh, don't worry. The fire will never come into Centralia." All we could do was pray that it wouldn't come near us.

We had lots of fun growing up in Centralia. You wouldn't think that us coal crackers would have a good time in a small town like this, but we did. People in Centralia would give you their hearts. They were sweet and everybody worked together. Catholics and Protestants and all nationalities. Everybody that ever came to Centralia hated to go home. I had one cousin from Philadelphia who used to cry every time her vacation was over and she had to go home. Everything they ever did in this town they did with pep and ambition.

ELIZABETH GILLESPIE.

40

O<small>UR</small> <small>MONITOR NEVER</small> went off, thank God. We were glad that Wayne and Dennis would come in and examine the house. They'd tell us everything was okay.

Kit took everything from day to day, like the rest of us. You have to when you're in trouble like we were. Maybe you wouldn't get up one day, you'd be smothered.

The government did this. They started coming in and saying we'd have to go. We'd say, "Let the fire come and we'll block it out somehow." We never took it to heart until now. Everybody else in our family had moved away or died, so it was just Kit and me living in the house at the end. It broke our hearts. Then my sister, Kit, died, and it was like the meaning of the town just went out of it.

ELIZABETH GILLESPIE.
Gillespie moved to a nursing home in Dan-
ville, Pennsylvania, after her sister died.

Kit Kane watches as the Department of Environmental Resources inspector makes his
daily stop to check for gases in her home. Kit

passed away within weeks of relocating from
Centralia.

Brownie Troop No. 175 marches past a borehole on Memorial Day.

CENTRALIANS ARISE!

Speak out and defend your homes—your little town of Centralia is in danger. When one speaks of "home," they love it, even with all its imperfections, and are reluctant to leave it without serious reason.

Some homes are identified with certain families, generation after generation, and are a source of pride and love to them. You do not destroy your home because it needs to be repaired, and neither should Centralia be sacrificed because it has imperfections.

This is still America. Our forefathers came to this area, built this town, and enjoyed peace and religious freedom. We still want these rights and privileges, and under our democratic law we are entitled to them. We do not appreciate being harassed by the news media and government officials trying to relocate people and use the land for their own gain.

People should stop and think before they make any rash decisions. Think positive! This is a happy little town for many young and old alike. In most cities, how many can say that, where to walk on the street by day is as dangerous as it is at night? Do not be afraid; stand up and be counted for Centralia!

Where else but in Centralia will you find . . .

- A home that you own free and clear, remodeled just the way you always wanted it
- Churches nearby to comfort and sustain you
- A bank and a post office within walking distance, where old friends meet daily to pass some time
- Plenty of parking spaces
- Fresh air and usually good water
- Safety from floods, hurricanes, and tornadoes
- Freedom to walk the streets, day or night, without fear of muggings, rape, or harassment
- Children playing happily and safely
- Hospitals, ambulance service, schools, and factories that can be reached in a short time
- Minimal taxes compared to other areas
- In times of sickness or death, good neighbors who are there when you need them
- Sociological studies indicate that relocating the elderly can be fatal

FELLOW TOWNSMEN, CONSIDER ALL OF THE ABOVE BEFORE YOU SELL CENTRALIA SHORT OR EVEN THINK OF LEAVING! THE DANGER TO OUR TOWN HAS BEEN GROSSLY EXAGGERATED!

Residents to Save the Borough of Centralia fact sheets.

44

Mary Gallagher and her family scrapbook.

THAT NURSE LADY was around the other day, from the state. I said, "You go back and tell your boss that it's a heck of a time to be doing anything like a health study when it's time for the people to be leaving." I don't think that it's right to be taking it now. What good is it now when we're leaving? What good is it to us? She asked if I wanted the nurse to come back tomorrow and take a urine test and a blood test, and I said no. If I want that, I'll go to a doctor.

Certain days I feel that it has affected my health. Headaches. And some days, my legs and arms just won't go. Now mind you, I know that I'm old, but I know it has to be the gas, because I never felt just bleck like I do now. And the ticking of the monitor, that used to bother me terrible. And we had to pay for the electricity to keep the monitors going. It adds quite a bit to your bill. It's going all the time.

I would have liked to have seen the town saved. That's what the government should have done in the beginning. My backyard, where the gas vents are now, was all huckleberries. They called it the picnic grounds. Now, there are rocks burnt red as big as half of this room. It used to be beautiful. They bulldozed it. It's a bad dream I keep thinking I'll wake up from.

I'm supposed to decide whether to move in two months? Am I going to be ready? How do I know? Maybe I'll be dead. That would save me a lot of bother, wouldn't it?

MARY GALLAGHER, 82,
a lifelong resident of the impact zone across from St. Ignatius Church.

*Charlie Gasperetti in Eva Moran's
candy store.*

THE MINE FIRE stinks. I get headaches and my throat is clogged most of the winter-time. You're not allowed to go out and play because of it.

When I was a little kid, I thought Centralia was gonna be a nice place. There are lots of trees to have clubhouses. But when I was five or six, I realized that they weren't going to put the fire out. I swear I've seen ghosts coming out of the abandoned houses.

I don't want to move, but we have to because of the smoke. My friends and I wanted to get all the fire trucks and water tankers in the world and put the fire out.

CHARLIE GASPERETTI, 8.

MY HUSBAND JOE and I were there the very first day the fire started. It wasn't any bigger than this table. It was a real hot day and the sun was beating down. I thought maybe it was hot glass that set some paper on fire and that hit the coal, but others claim no, it wasn't that way. Everybody has their own opinion about it. Some claim that it was burning long before that.

We've lived in Centralia all our lives. Joe and I were born on the same street up in what's now the hot side. We've owned the confectionery store here on Locust Avenue for seventeen years. If it weren't for the mine fire, we'd never go. We have nice people comin' in the store, nice kids. I'll miss the kids.

You can't blame people for wanting to stay or wanting to go. It's just this everyday business—mine fire, mine fire. "Are you going? I'm not. Would you go? Yes, I'm goin'." It just makes the ones who don't want to go mad to hear you say that you're willing to go. I've lost friends from this. There's nothing I can do about it. If they don't want to talk to me, I can't make them.

EVA MORAN.
Concerned Citizens started around Moran's kitchen table.

*Department of Environmental Resources
inspector tests for gases in a kitchen sink.*

ON JULY 12, 1983, Centralians gathered at borough hall to hear the results of a long-awaited study conducted for the U.S. Department of the Interior on the mine fire.

They learned that, in a sense, the mine fire was terminal. The fire was spreading faster, and the potential area of risk was far greater, than anyone had previously thought. A possible thirty-seven hundred acres including Centralia and several other communities would be at risk if the fire were allowed to burn itself out, a process that could take more than a century.

Of the engineering options suggested, the only foolproof method would be total excavation of the affected area—at a prohibitive cost of $660 million. The preferred method would include a series of trenches to isolate the fire. The trenches, at a cost of approximately $100 million, would be five hundred feet deep and twelve hundred feet across, and would effectively destroy the quality of life in Centralia. Residents would be subjected to around-the-clock digging, blasting, noise, and dirt. Floating particulate matter from the trenching could be more hazardous to health than the mine fire. Additionally, there remains the possibility that the fire could jump the site of the proposed trench, rendering it useless once work was begun.

As U.S. Representative Frank Harrison, whose district includes Centralia, stated, "It turns out that James Watt was right when he said the fire would eventually burn itself out. Unfortunately, that will take a century or two and one town and two small villages would be rendered uninhabitable."

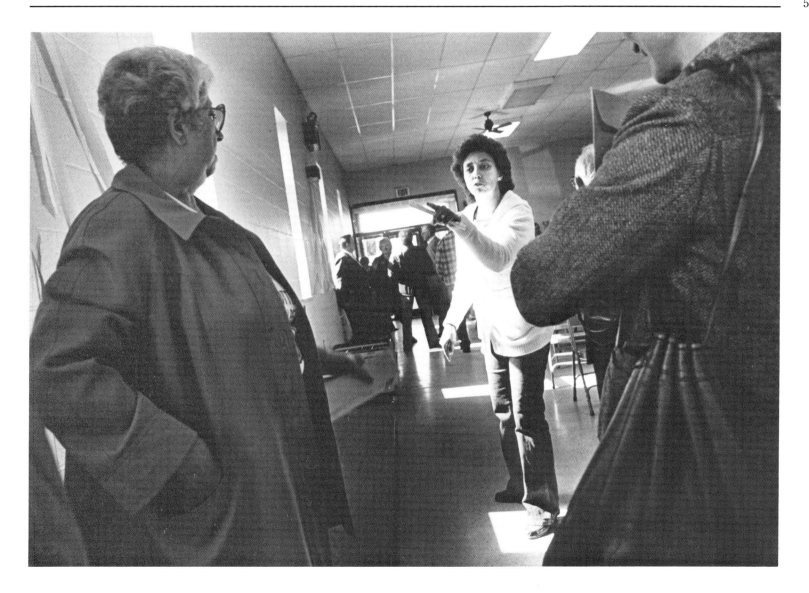

58

THINGS WERE TOUGH when I was growing up in Centralia, but it was a good town, a close town. During the depression years, it was hard on everybody. During the coal strikes, nobody was employed. In the summer, families would go pick wild huckleberries and they would supplement their income that way. Families also had their own independent coal holes, and they would mine the coal and prepare it themselves to sell to bootleg truckers.

I ran away to New York around 1934, when I was fifteen. I had been working in a coal hole. One day me and a friend finally had enough, so we just threw down our shovels and took off. It was hard work for kids. It was all manual labor. You had to bring the coal up by hand with a windless hoist. Then you'd have to sit down with the hammer and smash it into correct sizes to prepare it for market. We worked eight, ten, sometimes twelve hours a day. One day we just started hitchhiking. I finally got a job as a bellhop running errands in the Radio City complex. Later I joined the military.

I advanced into administrative positions and became the cemetery superintendent at Arlington National Cemetery. We lived inside the cemetery when President Kennedy was assassinated. I was in charge of all the field operations and burials, so I was actually the one who had the responsibility of preparing the grave. When President Kennedy was buried, we had twenty-two individuals that day before him. All were buried on time without any interruptions. When I retired, they gave me the shovel that we had used to dig Kennedy's grave.

My children were raised all over the country. They really can't claim a hometown. I feel they were deprived of something that was here. Centralia was a good place to raise kids, but there just wasn't any opportunity for them anymore. I remember Centralia when there were numerous stores, a big department store, an A&P. When my dad came over from what was then Austria (now Russia) in 1910, it was a booming little coal town. There was plenty of work all around during the boom years of the coal industry. So this is home, and there was a real pull to retire here.

If anybody asks me where I'm from, I just say where I came from is no more. They're taking my home away; it'll be gone. My children didn't have a hometown because they traveled, but my hometown existed. I lived in it. I grew up in it and came back to it to retire. Now it's gone.

METRO "METCH" KOWALCHICK.

Metro Kowalchick.

I STARTED MY army career in Hawaii with stopovers in Panama and Puerto Rico. We lived all over the place. Philadelphia; Winchester, Virginia; Louisville, Kentucky; Ft. Leavenworth, Texas; Ft. Lee, Virginia; Ft. Knox, Kentucky. But Centralia's home; it's where my roots are. I never thought of it any other way. The person that sold us this home had lived here all her life, and she was eighty.

I retired back here in 1979. That was right around when the mine fire was gaining attention. We were curious about it, so some friends took us up to the top of town and showed us where it was burning. We didn't give it much thought. We had considered building right near the fire by the Odd Fellows Cemetery. We thought the fire was isolated in that area, so we thought we'd be safe in the center of town.

My feelings changed when people started complaining about gases in their homes. I didn't doubt that there could be gases in the homes because that whole area is undermined. I remember when I was a boy, our church, SS. Peter and Paul Orthodox on Park Street, caved in, and there was nothing but coal under there. They filled it back up and the church was saved. That was around 1932. I was a young boy, and I remember going to church one Sunday and seeing the big hole there. You'd look down into the void and see coal there.

I found it hard to believe that the fire started from burning trash. I could never start a coal fire from the top. I always had to start one from the bottom. Even if you started a fire on the top and there was coal under there, it wouldn't burn. I think that the fire was burning a long time before people knew about it. I've talked to miners who say it could've come from the Bast Mines or Collieries down by Big Mine Run about a mile from where the fire was discovered. It could have been going for thirty years before they discovered it.

If it weren't for the idea of a trench, we'd stay. At the town meeting in July, the study revealed how the fire was advancing, and it seems definite that they are going to dig a trench to contain it. I don't see how anybody could live in Centralia if they go through with digging that trench. I definitely feel it's unfair that they're not being specific about what they're going to do to contain the fire. If you stay, you take your chances. I feel like I'm being forced to leave.

METRO KOWALCHICK.

64

WHEN THE SMOKE comes over your house, that's enough to scare anybody. The doctor told me to get out in the wintertime, 'cause that's when the smoke is the worst. I was usually an active person all day. I would come in in the afternoon and sit on a recliner, and the first thing you know I could feel my eyes dropping. So it had to be from the gas, because it was something I never did before in all my life.

I been living here all my life, but I'd be plenty scared living here now. 'Cause that gas line is right outside our pavement there. And if the fire ever hits that, that's what I would be dreading. We'd be blown to bits.

My children moved out when they got married. Robert was still living at home when the fire was starting to get bad. Then he got work in Harrisburg, and he moved to Middletown. And he had just built a new home when Three Mile Island happened. He was only three miles away from that. I called him and said, "You get up home! Get away from that area!"

I never thought it would come to this. I thought that in time they would find something that would be able to control the fire. The material that they had used three times straight, the fly ash, didn't help one bit. I thought that in time, if they built the trench, it would outten the fire.

MARY TYSON, 70.
Tyson lived all her life in Centralia. She eventually moved to California to be near her son.

Mary Tyson next to the carbon monoxide monitor in her living room.

WAYNE AND DENNIS, those boys from DER, are two of the nicest guys you would ever want to have come into your home. Because if you had any problem, any situation that you couldn't handle in your home, they were there, ready to help. They are the two grandest guys. I never felt it was an intrusion, because I always felt that they were there for our safety.

MARY TYSON.

Wayne Readly, a Department of Environmental Resources inspector, testing for gases in Mary Tyson's bedroom.

I'VE LIVED HERE in this house all my life, and this is quite upsetting. I'm told that the fire is almost out now and that they haven't had any gas readings in a year and that there's no danger in it coming down here. But I'm not a technician or a geologist or what have you.

We've never had any gases, but I think people that did had good reason to leave. If we were in danger of any kind, if we had gases, I wouldn't have to be told by any-body. That would be my first priority. Out. No matter how much I like it.

We've talked to a lot of people who have moved and they're trying to adjust, but there's no place like Centralia. The bottom line is that they miss it. We have nothing fabulous here except the quality of the people. It's the people that makes the town. Everybody knows everybody, even their animals. We don't have drugs, robberies, or rapes. You can't buy happiness, and I guess people belong where they're happy.

If the government would have said that this was a disaster, which they never did, we would have accepted that willingly. But the government has never said that we were a disaster and forced relocation. I think if there was a fire, and it was serious, we'd be ordered out of Centralia. We wouldn't be sitting here. The United States is very powerful, and I'm certain, with the technology that they have today, if this was serious, it would be put out. They're helping other countries, and I believe that charity begins at home. If you're gonna do something for somebody, you start right at home.

MOLLY DARRAH,
president of the Centralia Borough Council. Darrah lives in the center of town with her bedridden sister, Winnie.

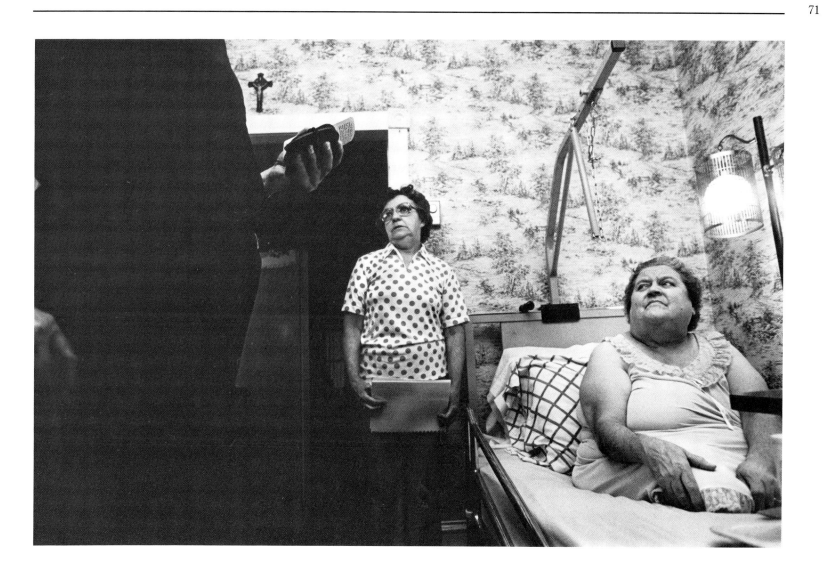

I'M NOT WORRIED about the fire because I figure that if something is going to happen, it's just plain meant to be. There's always something that could happen.

We don't have a monitor. If I've had a bad night with the kids, sometimes I just let the doorbell ring when they come around to check for gases.

I grew up on a farm, and I got used to the pesticides so the gases don't bother me. The only time we can smell them is when the wind shifts. It's just as hazardous as anything else. When the stoker kicked back sulfur, that registered when they tested for gas. When the eucs [heavy mining equipment] were running back and forth when my husband, Jimmy, was a kid and they were stripping, that threw coal dust into the air. It's just a fact of life.

LINDA TARLECKI, 21,
mother of two and resident of Byrnesville.

Linda Tarlecki and son, Jimmy, 6 months.

Linda and Jimmy Tarlecki.

I'D LIKE TO STAY. I enjoy living in Byrnesville. There isn't much traffic, and I never worry about the kids.

When they close the road into Centralia, it's a real pain 'cause all the traffic comes through Byrnesville. We'd have to go around to Ashland to get our mail. It could add twenty minutes to what was a five-minute trip.

I'd like to raise the kids here. We're related to nine or ten houses out of the twenty-one down here.

LINDA TARLECKI.

I'D GO TO ALL the weddings and take photographs and give them to people as a wedding present. Now that it seems that the end is coming, it's nice to see everybody together 'cause there are fewer and fewer happy occasions.

PATSY "TINY" KLINE.

Helen Womer addressing a borough council meeting.

THE FIRE HAS not destroyed this community. The government has. Sensationalism by the press has. Radical elements within our community have—people who had access to newspapers and television stations. We were not organized enough in time. Because we are the working people, I don't think we ever realized it would get this far.

We are not suffering from the fire. We have not suffered one day. Psychologically, maybe from the controversy, but not from the fire. We don't have a monitor in our house. And I'm a "hot-sider." As hot as you can get. It's always been my contention that most of these readings were not from mine fire gas at all. They're just from everyday living. Time and time again you read that a closed home is more detrimental to people's health than anything that they could pick up outside. It's heartbreaking to see what's happening to this town, but we are determined to preserve our community.

Our group is just what the name implies—to save the borough. Nobody can come in here and say we're not a community and try and rape us of all our coal. We will have weathered a storm unlike any other American probably has ever weathered. We will be steeled. Every crisis you go through in life, I feel, makes you stronger.

I've seen people get involved in Centralia for their own benefit—the opportunists. The people that didn't own houses and got involved with trying to destroy Centralia. It will never be the same. The part that is hard for me is that I have to deal with the very people that were instrumental in destroying the town. I work in a bank, and I have to be civil and courteous when my heart is breaking.

We will be closer—the ones that are left—than we were as a whole town. Because we will have given up government big bucks to stay. I'm convinced there will still be a community. Unless something unforeseen on a higher level happens. At this point, I can't see anything that would convince us to go. There's no need to go. If the mine fire flared up, if these temperatures got up to seven or eight or nine hundred degrees, then it would be time to go. It's got to be nine hundred degrees to burn anthracite coal. You have to have specific conditions to spontaneously ignite gases, and those conditions don't exist here. If our cellar had gas in it, our fire would go out because we heat our home with coal.

I'm going to stay as long as it's safe and hopefully be a strength to somebody who needs it. Money isn't everything.

HELEN WOMER,
Residents to Save the Borough of Centralia.

THE ONLY VISIBLE sign that there is a fire close to Centralia is along Route 61 down from St. Ignatius Church. And that can never come this way because the church is built on solid rock. Any miner will tell you that. If the fire goes anywhere, it will go across the street and out that way. You could walk two thousand feet to the outcrop and that would be the end of it.

The heat is emanating from somewhere else, but they don't know where because they never went off far enough to find it. Some of the boreholes that have recorded abnormally high temperatures are now normal. Maybe James Watt was right after all. Granted, he had foot-in-mouth disease. But maybe what he said pertaining to Centralia was true. This could all be analyzed and everything could be explained.

When we had those horrendous conditions of steam and stench and smoke up in that area during the winter of 1983 we went to DER [Department of Environmental Resources] and asked that something be done. Well, the Office of Surface Mining had promised that DER could take money from the Abandoned Mine Reclamation Fund to do something. They said they were going to look into it. And still nothing's been done. Because that's the only proof for photographers, for newspeople. They come in and see the smoke and say, "Well, no wonder. That's great of the government to want to help get the people out of Centralia." But remember, there has never been a crisis, never a disaster, never an emergency declared in Centralia. Never.

HELEN WOMER.

Charlie Gasperetti, Sam Garula (center),
and Trish Catizone at a meeting of the
Centralia Committee for Human Development.

I JOINED THE Concerned Citizens right after I graduated from high school. I got very involved; and when the original officers resigned, they nominated me to be president. I was twenty then. I was scared but we needed somebody to keep the group above water and I didn't want to let anybody down. We set up an office and initiated the thirty-thousand-dollar grant that brought Honor Murphy into town and started the Centralia Committee for Human Development.

I learned that the government really isn't fair to the small people. You have to have an awful lot of people to make a difference to the government. They might pretend that they're listening to you, but they're not. I think we fought pretty well for the number of people we had. I also realized there are a lot of narrow-minded people in the coal region. They can really be ostriches and stick their heads in the sand and say that nothing is wrong when it's right in front of their eyes. I couldn't just sit by and watch.

When you have something in common to fight for, I can't believe how close it brings you to the people you're working with. I didn't mind going to the meetings. It got to the point where I would look forward to the meetings because I felt like I was accomplishing something. Nobody came up to you and said, "Nice job," besides the people you worked with.

I got along fine with my neighbors until I started opening my mouth, saying that we needed to be relocated. I wasn't trying to tell them that they had to move. I was just saying that I wanted to be relocated because I felt it was dangerous living in Centralia.

TRISH CATIZONE, 23,
former president of Concerned Citizens.

THE ONLY THING that resolves problems of this sort is people banding together. When you look at Love Canal, it wasn't the fact that 56 percent of the babies were born birth-defected that initiated our evacuation. It was an election campaign. That's the way the system works. The media is the only way to move public officials to do what's right, and the media reacts to mothers and children. Politicians know that. The only way to stop companies is economic. Dow, Hooker, or Union Carbide: If they don't pay, they're going to continue to do what they're doing. They don't have morals, they don't have principles. They only know profit. Once you affect their profit, then they'll change.

In Times Beach it had absolutely nothing to do with the fact that they were exposed to dioxin. That evacuation came solely because Ann Gorsuch and Rita Lavelle's heads were on the chopping block. Love Canal, Times Beach, and now Centralia are all major public embarrassments.

The people who are fighting with political action, with voices, with togetherness and common sense are winning. The first thing that people think they need to do is hire a lawyer. The second thing is to go get a hydrologist or a toxicologist. That is such a wrong move. They don't need to hire experts. It wastes money, and people have to realize that these are not scientific issues, but political issues. Nobody knows what the mine fire gas is going to do to folks over a twenty-year period. Or dioxin. You can't argue it scientifically; therefore, you can't argue it legally. There is no such thing as objective science when politics is involved.

Even though we were winging it in Love Canal and learning from the seat of our pants, we did well because we knew what we were doing politically. The hardest thing to convince people of is that their families' dying from toxic exposure, be it from mine fire gas or dioxin, is not going to get them out. And women will say, "No, no, no, I can't organize, I'm not a Lois Gibbs." And I'll say, "Of course you are." What's a Lois Gibbs? A Lois Gibbs is a housewife. Any housewife in America knows how to organize, budget, and delegate responsibility. And women tend to be highly involved in grass-roots organizing. Disasters seem to hit low- to moderate-income, minority, blue-collar communities where the men are working all the time on swing shifts. The country club communities usually escape. And the government plays on their feelings of powerlessness by telling the people that they're not experts, they've never gone to college, and they're just dumb housewives. If the bureaucracy would give people straight information, the amount of emotional stress would be much less. Instead they say, "We have these Ph.D.'s, this consulting firm, and we're going to do this health study and that survey," and people just feel like guinea pigs.

But there's no way the "scientists" are objective with all these dollar signs looking them in the face. You have to realize the bureaucrats initiating the studies are also going to be paying for the resolution to the problem. The same is true of people from universities doing studies, because their funding generally comes from the state or corporations. They're going to do a twenty-million-dollar study on Love Canal. For what? They're trying to revitalize it and sell the homes.

LOIS GIBBS,
former Love Canal activist and executive director of Citizen's Clearinghouse for Hazardous Waste.

Members of the Centralia Committee for Human Development [CCHD] listen to Lois Gibbs's radio address. Gibbs was being interviewed in another room of the CCHD office.

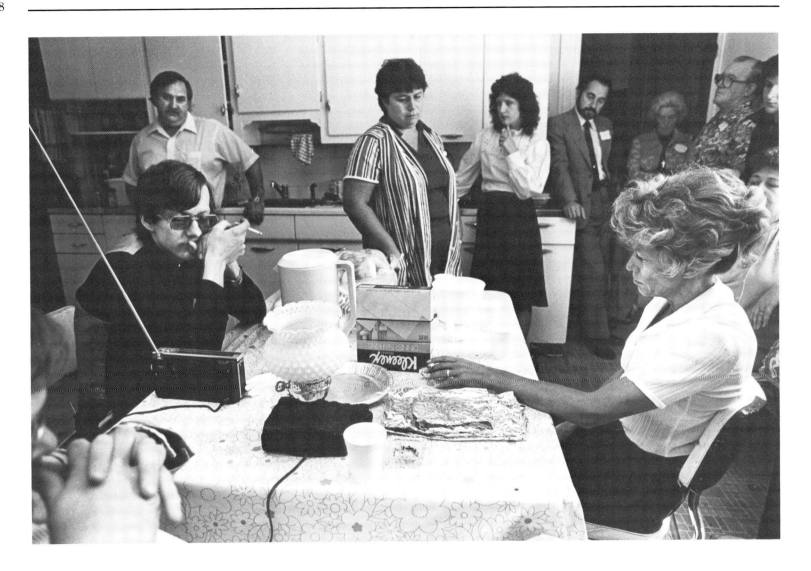

I USED TO THINK, God, look what I'm going through. What they went through in Love Canal was ten times worse. At the end of Lois Gibbs's speech, I was practically in tears. She gave us a burst of initiative to keep fighting.

TRISH CATIZONE.

WE LEARNED FROM Lois to try not to get frustrated. Just keep plugging as long as you believe that what you're doing is right. My problem with all of this was that I got too absorbed. For almost two years I lived, breathed, and ate mine fire. Every waking moment that was not spent at work was spent talking about it, on the phone, in someone's office, or with the media. I burned myself out. But for a small group, we did a hell of a lot.

TOMMY LARKIN.

CENTRALIA PUT A lot of strain on my marriage—like Love Canal did to Lois. Our house wasn't safe, our environment wasn't safe. My two little girls were always sick. I looked to my husband to take care of everything, but there was nothing he could do.

I wasn't sure that we needed to get out, just something to make us safer. I felt victimized, but working to help people get away from the fire helped me to grow up a lot. It made me see there was more that I would like to do than stay home and take care of the kids, even though they're still my number one priority.

I learned how to cope with problems and trust my own decisions. Before Centralia I felt people used to hype these things up out of nothing. Now I'm easily drawn to people's plights. If they start up Three Mile Island again, they'll probably have to drag me off the gates.

CATHARENE JURGILL, 22,
mother of two and former treasurer of Concerned Citizens.

I sit in my window and watch the snowfall turning to steam
I curse the fire that has burned through my dream.
The damp road, snow falling, steam rising, traffic proceeding
toward the setting sun, an eerie sight they be, here in Centralia
as the nightmare worsens, as the ticking intensifies each
evening,
monitoring the air I
breathe
I am poisoned by a silent enemy.
There is no escape from the ticking.
So perched on my windowsill I seethe.
People passing don't see the fire that burns.
Underground—my skin playing a game—that I can't win
I want to leave—I've nowhere to go—the fire burns deeper—
until it scorches my very soul.
My life is bitter, here on this hellish earth.
When tragic reminders of the happiness I'd planned
The one brown leaf that clings to the tree—
I am it and it is me
We might as well both be damned.

CATHARENE JURGILL.

I KNEW THE FIRE was bad, mostly for the children. It was definitely affecting them. It affected Catharene—stress and strain, worrying about the kids, cave-ins. You know how men are—stubborn and relatively calm.

What Catharene did—working on all the groups—was constructive. I only wished that she had used her talents for some other cause.

It's a shame. A town that was so close and now it's so torn. Neighbors disagree. My parents are basically undecided about what to do. We had the common sense to move. A lot of older people couldn't do that. We moved on our own before any money was allocated. We knew the children's health was endangered. So we scraped the money together and I worked two jobs.

It all gave me some gray hairs. Probably aged me five years.

LEON JURGILL, 28.
The Jurgills later separated.

Catharene and Leon Jurgill and their
daughter, Katrina, 5.

IF I HAD been living up close to the fire like my sister, Catharene, was, yes, that would have been a big problem there. She had problems through her pregnancy with her daughter, living right on top of the fumes, and the doctors didn't know what the outcome was going to be from breathing all those gases. The baby could have been born with a lot of different lung problems and things, they said.

Where she lived, there's danger. Immediate danger. I noticed mood changes in her. She was always sick. We used to have our private discussions about the politics and all that, but I was too afraid to just speak out like she did. She went public with it, and she got interested in all the committees, and I just kind of sat back because my husband was born and raised in Centralia. And he felt kind of like her husband, that it wasn't endangering us that much.

My sister was put under a lot of stress. I wasn't very considerate of her feelings. I couldn't understand her being tired all the time until I was spending a lot of time up there and I would feel the same way. But I never looked at her and said, "Well, now I understand."

COLLEEN RUSSEN, 20,
talking about her sister, Catharene Jurgill.

Catharene Jurgill rests her hand against her sister, Colleen, pregnant with her first child.

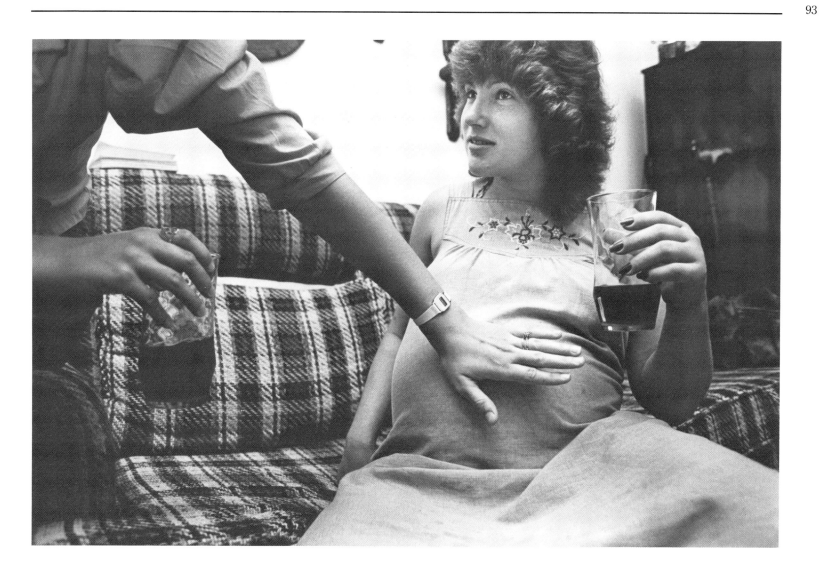

*Colleen and John Russen in the hospital
maternity ward.*

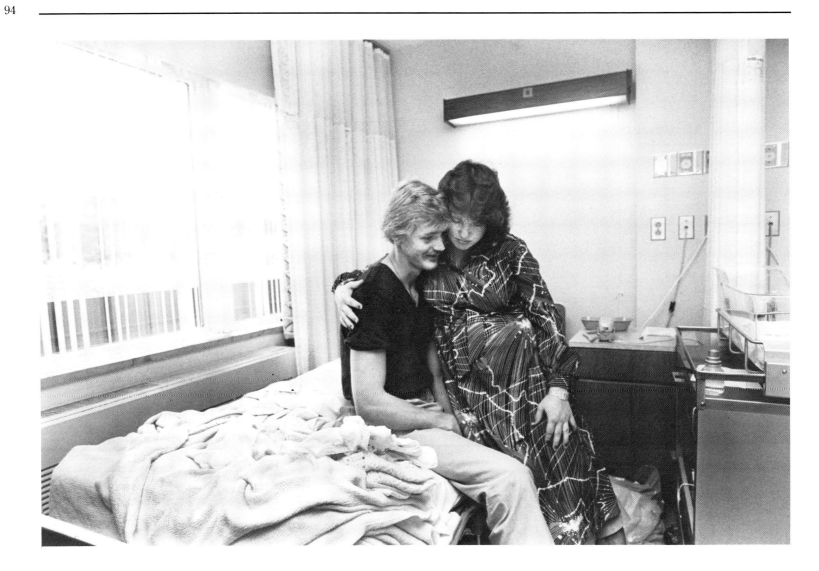

WE MOVED IN next to my mother-in-law two years ago. Our house was in really rough shape when we moved in. My husband, being a carpenter, fixed it up, put in all new walls and plumbing, electrical work, and ripped out staircases and stuff. Initially the home was given to John when his father died, but the transaction was never taken care of on paper, so the house is still in his mother's name. I'm a little scared. Since the home isn't in our name, we won't be getting relocation money. So what we get for our home—that's it. We've sunk over eleven thousand dollars into it—that's without any carpenter's costs. John works as a security guard and a carpenter on the side, and I work at Dino's Beauty Salon in Frackville.

I feel very fortunate to own a home at the age of twenty and to have it fixed up very beautiful. I'm also worried what we'll get for the house. People in the towns around Centralia have stuck the prices of their homes for sale up outrageously, because they know that the people from Centralia will be looking and they will be in demand.

My home has sentimental value to it because my husband did it all by himself for me. We both worked on it, but he gave up more for it than I did. He sold off guns and bows and weights and things so it would be ready for us to move into. In a way that hurt me, to see him sell off the things that meant the most. But then I also knew that he was doing it for us. It showed me a lot of love.

To go and leave that home with all the love that was put into it, that's the only thing that hurts me.

COLLEEN RUSSEN.

I KEPT LOOKING down and thinking, "That's my little girl!" I didn't worry about bringing her back and the mine fire. It wasn't bothering us and it probably never will affect anybody down at our end of town. But then again I was born and raised here, so the fire was always there. There was no sense worrying about it. I'm twenty-four, and I've been here since the time that I was born and it never affected me.

JOHN RUSSEN,
in the hospital after the birth of his first child,
Irene.

John Russen watching his newborn
daughter, Irene.

A monitor measures the air for carbon monoxide while Chrissie Kogut, 14, sits in her brother's bedroom.

I'D LIKE TO LIVE in Centralia, but I hate the gases. I'd get headaches and the monitor went off. It went off at school and we'd have to leave.

My teachers and everybody would always ask me about the fire. I just tell them it's a living hell. I did mostly all my school reports on it. I went up to the DER office, and Dennis gave me tubes and papers from the monitors and stuff.

You get so used to the monitor ticking that sometimes you don't even remember it's there until it goes off. It didn't go off many times. I was never scared because they were all false alarms, except maybe once or twice when the gases were really high. We'd just let it go off. You get used to it, even when the gases are high. You've gotta die sometime.

I'd like to stay. All my friends are here. Everybody babysits for everybody else. We were one big happy family. I wished I got to know the town better. Even though it's small, you don't really know a town until you know everybody in it.

CHRISSIE KOGUT, 14.
Chrissie lived on a block of Locust Avenue in the impact zone where children had high rates of upper respiratory problems.

*Joan Girolami addresses a Centralia
Borough Council meeting.*

CONCERNED CITIZENS STARTED toward the end of 1979. We started in Eva Moran's kitchen. There were fifteen or twenty of us, and we went to the borough council and asked if we could have that one small room, and we had to fight for that. Those first Concerned Citizens meetings were terrible. We didn't know what we were doing. There was a lot of fighting. Nobody wanted to take the officers' seats. It was really tough going.

When we organized Concerned Citizens, we were really fighting for a project to put the fire out. We felt that a project might save some of the town, and that's what we were looking out for. The monitors were already there, but then they came back and told us that they didn't know where the fire was, so they couldn't give us a project to put it out. They had to have the boreholes first!

Our congressman wanted the boreholes, Helen Womer wanted the boreholes, so we thought, "Well, if this is the way to show the people there's really a problem here, we'll go for the boreholes!" So we went for the boreholes. And we found the fire in the borough. But still people didn't believe it. They didn't want to believe it.

When we started, we had all this energy, all this strength. We were going to do everything! Up and go to Harrisburg, Washington, and write politicians. We felt like the Great Crusaders! Slowly, everybody just let us down. They just didn't have the time. They were busy with their own lives. Some of the people were moving out of town. The borehole study and the thirty-thousand-dollar grant from the Catholic Church to es-

tablish the Centralia Committee for Human Development and bring Sister Honor Murphy into town were really all we could get through. We were just worn down.

Nobody in the town wanted the Concerned Citizens, it seemed. Sometimes I wondered why we even bothered to try and help. Council didn't want us, yet council didn't want to do anything. The people didn't want us, but the people didn't want to do anything. Made you wonder. Not facing the problem wasn't going to make it go away. It's there. . . .

JOAN GIROLAMI, 42,
former vice president of Concerned Citizens.

I THINK IT was a slow buildup of government lies and hot temperatures that got me. In the beginning I was apathetic, like everyone else. In 1969 they drilled holes in my yard and told me there was no fire there. So I forgot about it.

We wanted to put in a pool, so we went to the Bureau of Mines and asked if the fire was there. And they said, "No, no, no, go ahead and put the pool in." So we spent a couple thousand dollars and put a pool in. Then they put in more boreholes and found the temperature in my backyard was seven hundred degrees. I was furious, and I had never gotten anything in writing from them when they told me it was safe.

The real truth about how bad it is in Centralia never surfaced. Pennsylvania Emergency Management Agency got involved, and they were ready for a big disaster and evacuation. But we were never told that. We had to practically steal their records and hurry up and ship them back and not say where we got them.

I got threatened on the phone. Nasty letters. They firebombed Dave Lamb's place. Some guy painted a hex sign on the street in front of my house. He said it was a hex on the government for not putting the fire out.

JOAN GIROLAMI.

Joan Girolami.

MY ROOTS IN Centralia go back to the Civil War. My great-uncle was the first boy in Centralia to become a priest. My mother was once in a convent. In the acquisition of 1981, they took my homestead. They boarded up the homes, then they sprayed them with red number twos, since that was the second acquisition. It was a real tough time for everybody. When that's your ancestors' house, and when there's no physical damage done to it, it's very hard to accept that a perfect home is being demolished for no reason at all.

I have a lot of anger inside me when I walk by my grandmother's old homestead. If I had a government official, I would have kicked him in the rear for all the years, all they've put the people through. If they'd just have done something sooner, we would have what we've lost. We would still have it. It is a case of a small town that people just don't care about. You could cry out for help all you wanted, but it wouldn't go past a fifteen-mile radius. It wasn't until Todd fell into the subsidence that it got national attention, and they realized something needed to be done. That was the turning point.

I was always taught that in times of trouble a priest was someone that you could always go to. I found it very difficult when Father McGinley came out stressing the spiritual and historic value of Centralia, and not the health and safety of the people. During Easter Mass we were in line to receive communion from him, and I pulled little Charlie out of that line and went to the other. I couldn't receive communion from him. I would have been a hypocrite. I feel like I've lost my church.

Most of his group, the Residents to Save the Borough of Centralia group, lives in the safe part of town. They have no right to say there are no ill side effects. It isn't any easier for us to leave than it would be for the people who want to stay, but we have to put our health and safety first. That doesn't mean that we don't care about the spiritual and historic. We have to move for our sanity.

MARY GASPERETTI, 33.

The Gasperetti family on Easter Sunday.

Mary and Jenny Gasperetti, 4.

Jenny Gasperetti.

WE'VE HAD RESPIRATORY problems that were just endless. I had serious stress problems and started taking Valium like a lot of the women in town. I met with a group of women every week at the Family Counseling and Mental Health Clinic. I let out a lot of anxiety, and realized that it's okay to be afraid.

MARY GASPERETTI.

Mary and Jenny Gasperetti.

Mary and Jenny Gasperetti.

Father Anthony McGinley.

110

YOU ALWAYS SEE the flame drawings with stories on Centralia. There are no flames. Tourists come and want to know where the house is burning up. Not one house has ever burned or come close to burning. We just get that dull smoke and fog on a rainy day, which could be removed if they used a little of the money they are wasting. I think it's overplayed. We feel that the fire could be excavated in nothing flat! Three or four days! I think most people will admit there's a fire somewhere, but I do firmly believe that most of us think it's no threat. Of course, the children of the 200 block of Locust Avenue reported upper respiratory problems. They were told to. I'm sure they're all cured now. They're getting their money. The little boy who fell in the "fire" over there, well, we can show you where the Mt. Carmel paper published an article in 1894 stating that the people should move from Locust Avenue because it was thoroughly and completely undermined and that there would be subsidences. Eventually there were. The kid fell in, but that wasn't the fire. There are subsidences everywhere there are coal mines. What do you think a coal mine is?

Our group surfaced when we saw the whole scramble and despair and all the money, yet nothing to put the fire out. This is where the proposed trench was such a nightmare, a mere fancy, and a scare tactic used to get people to move out. They kept scaring the hell out of people with this trench idea, that they were going to have to live with trenches and the whole trenching process. The people in town would ask me, "What are we going to do, Father?" I asked them what they wanted to do. And they said, "Well, we have to get out." So I went home and thought it over. Do they have to get out? They don't have to get out.

This was never considered a disaster area. They were not forced out. They were given a voluntary choice. They are given fair market value for their homes as is. If it was a disaster area, they would have to be given replacement value, which is quite a bit more. So it's not a disaster area; they don't have to move, so sit tight. You do not have to leave. If there is some intrigue as to the ownership of the mineral rights underneath the town, as rumored, you're not losing any value by staying. If they are really after the fabulous value of our anthracite coal in the Mammoth Vein, as quite a few say, the day will come when you can get anything you want for a home to get you out of here. It won't be worth twenty-seven or thirty thousand dollars. You'll be able to name your buck. As owners of the borough, we own the mineral rights underneath it, and that's written into the deeds. No matter what they do, they can't change that, but, boy, have they tried.

We have a committee to look into seedlings and beautifying the town. We've already taken a step ahead on that. They will not be allowed to have boarded-up buildings. They will have to be razed. Grass must be planted and kept up. This town could be a beautiful park. When the people that are going are gone, and the houses are razed, and the grass grows again, I think Centralia will settle into a nice little hamlet.

FATHER ANTHONY McGINLEY, PH.D., 65.
Born in Centralia, Father McGinley moved elsewhere to study for the priesthood. After teaching at Georgetown University, he moved back to Centralia in 1982 and helped found Residents to Save the Borough of Centralia. When the house he rented in town was sold, he moved to nearby Germanville.

ALL OF THE OTHER disasters I've worked with have been natural disasters, particularly floods. This is the first time I've ever dealt with a technical disaster. A whole different thing happens here. I would not believe this if I were not currently living through it, seeing what happens to people in a disaster of this kind. In a natural disaster, everyone loses their house, everybody loses everything. So you put on the boots and you pitch in and you help and you eat bologna sandwiches that the Red Cross brings in. People are together. People are concerned. Now if there was a house fire in town, or a funeral, the people rally round. 'Cause those are human, natural disasters. But this other thing, I believe, has tended to divide people.

We'd like to try and preserve some of the community. We're looking at a gorgeous tract of land, about seven miles from Centralia. It's all oak trees. What we're hoping to put in there is a community development where the people would have control and really build a strong community there. If we can get some of this last resort housing money to assist in the development of the property, then we can afford to pay ten thousand dollars for a lot and put us up a nice little thirty-five- to thirty-eight-thousand-dollar house. If the Residents to Save the Borough really want to stay here and preserve this town, that's their right. But that reality is gone.

We've been in communication with the folks at Times Beach, Missouri, who have been through this. They either didn't pursue their community relocation hard enough, or they didn't have the leadership that knew how to work in among the agencies. They lost it. They're scattered. And what we hear from them is this: Don't let it happen to you. So the Centralia Committee for Human Development has formed a Homeowners Association to make sure that it doesn't.

SISTER HONOR MURPHY, 75,
project director of the Centralia Committee for Human Development. A Dominican nun for more than fifty years, Sister Murphy has worked with communities facing disasters since 1972.

On August 11, 1983, the residents of Centralia voted 345 to 200 in a nonbinding referendum to seek government assistance to buy their homes and allow them to relocate. Mayor John Wondoloski announces the vote.

IT WAS REALLY hectic the day of the referendum. I was at the municipal building from seven in the morning until after midnight. The referendum was a private ballot for homeowners. Anybody that owned a home was entitled to vote. If a homeowner's wife's name was on the deed, they got two votes. However many names were on the deed, that's how many votes they got. The first referendum had just been a show of hands at a public meeting.

It basically came out two-to-one that the residents wanted to go, but I think a lot of people voted that had empty houses. Some of that property wasn't even livable, so I don't think it was a true picture of the people in Centralia. Some of the people probably visited the town only once in three or four years.

When I went outside with the results, I saw a whole mob of people and lights and TV cameras and microphones and I thought, jeez, this looks like the presidential election. I felt like I was out there forever. And that was only the beginning. I was interviewed on "Nightline" that night.

I felt I had to read the results. The president of council could have done it, but I was putting all my time into this. I wasn't doing a hit-or-miss job here. I felt if anyone was going to announce it, I was. I didn't feel good announcing the vote to a town that's a hundred and some years old and has a lot of memories. Everyone was telling me that I was going to be the last mayor of Centralia and that's sad. But when you're a politician, you have to be able to shrug that off and go with the tide.

Had the Residents to Save the Borough group been vocal earlier, maybe this thing would have gone the other way. They were definitely the silent majority; they just started too late. They're in favor of getting this fire out—not just buy me a house and move me out.

Had the clergy, the different clubs, the fire company, the Legion, or some of the citizens come up here and put a little more effort into it, who knows? But you threaten people with a big trench coming through the middle of town and this is what happens. I think the idea of a trench is a scare tactic. There's nothing on the drawing board about it. If they put a trench in, I'd be the first one to tell you to go. They'd use eminent domain and tell you you're going and you'd go. But I think the trench is a joke. And the fire's gonna keep spreading.

MAYOR JOHN WONDOLOSKI.

On November 18, 1983, a busload of Centralians rode to Washington, D.C., to witness the signing of the appropriation bill enabling them to sell their homes and relocate.

Members of the Homeowners Association, waiting in the Capitol Building in Washington for the Congress to vote on a forty-two- million-dollar appropriation to pay for the relocation of Centralia residents.

MEMBERS OF THE Centralia Homeowners Association and Congress celebrated the passage of the forty-two-million-dollar appropriation bill by cutting a red ribbon symbolizing the government red tape they had finally managed to overcome.

I THINK IT'S great what the media has done. They have the power to change a lot of decisions. If it weren't for them, everything would have been all hushed up. They didn't let the government ignore the problem. I'd like to be able to do that for someone some day.

But it's not just the media that's gotta do it. It's the people. They just have to wake up and smell the coffee.

TODD DOMBOSKI.

NOT QUITE HALF the town wanted to go. I think this town could have been saved, but it wasn't. I think the publicity swung it. . . .

MAYOR JOHN WONDOLOSKI.

The first day government offers to purchase homes arrived at the Centralia Post Office.

The Mekosh house being appraised for government buy-out, with Stephen Mekosh, 11, and his cousin, Timmy, 15, on the couch.

I THINK IT finally sunk in the day of the appraisal. Stephen realized that we had to move. He understood that the fire was uptown and that it would come down eventually, but with the appraisal it really hit home.

He's upset with changing schools and losing his friends. He cries a lot in school and he's got the teachers crying. He's started to withdraw into himself and he's been under a doctor's care. Now he's on tranquilizers.

And it doesn't help to tell him that it's gonna get better after we move. We just have to wait and see.

FAYE MEKOSH,
wife of Sonny Mekosh (right). Sonny Mekosh, 45, has been a miner in Centralia since 1962 and still works the Seven Mountain vein under the town.

ALL WE EVER wanted was a chance to get on with our lives. I don't think that was too much to ask. I just want people to know how good this feels after all the hurt and bitterness. The reason the buy-out ceremony was so wonderful was because we finally got past the quarreling. People hugged me that had not spoken to me in over a year. It was a healing thing.

MARY GASPERETTI.
The Gasperettis built a new home in the west end of Mt. Carmel.

Mary Gasperetti at a public buy-out cere-
mony at borough hall on May 29, 1983.

SOME PEOPLE ARE very stoic about the whole thing. According to some of the health study interviews that we have access to, we're finding that some people are far more affected by the situation than you might think. The Department of Health will forward us a confidential letter and say that certain people are considered highest priority if you can accommodate them. Basically, it's because there are problems there. They don't mention what the problems are, but I have to take their word for it. Since they've been in town, a lot of that has shown up, really. There are some people that I deal with on a day-to-day basis and they showed up on the priority list, and while that has never come through to me, I'm certainly no trained psychologist either.

You either have to figure that the Department of Health doesn't know what they're doing or you seriously misjudged the person. I have to figure that the Department of Health knows what they're doing. So some of these people are hiding it on the surface pretty well, but evidently the fire and some of the other stresses involved are causing

some problems they're hiding from us very well anyway.

WILLIAM KLINK,
Columbia County Redevelopment Authority.
The Redevelopment Authority oversees the
forty-two-million-dollar relocation project in
Centralia.

Joan Girolami and Fran McKeefery listen as government representatives explain options for the government buy-out.

Joan Girolami.

I STARTED OFF as a housewife, going to the meetings and then getting so far involved that it was just about my whole life for a year. It got to be too much. When the Concerned Citizens got the thirty-thousand-dollar grant, I finally quit. I felt bad about that. I cried about that. I felt like I was giving up, just not helping the people. I was really afraid that somebody was going to die. At that point I was ready to break, and I did break.

I was smoking more than I ever was at the end there, I was so nervous. I was taking so many nerve pills I didn't know whether I was coming or going half the time. I was never on nerve pills my whole life until I got involved with this. One day I just took the pills in and dumped them on John's desk, at counseling, and he just said, "Oh my God, Joni, you can't keep taking these."

I got an ulcer, ended up having a lot of problems with my marriage, a lot of problems with my kids 'cause I was never there for them when I should have been. My Lori said to me, "You're looking at me, Mom, but I know you're not listenin'. You're thinkin' about the mine fire. You're away on trips half the time. You're never home. Doesn't the mine fire even quit on Sundays?"

JOAN GIROLAMI.

I'M SCARED. Hey, we're giving up our home, going back in debt. We hadn't had debts since 1964. So I can imagine how the elderly feel.

We got thirty-four thousand and fifteen thousand dollars for full relocation, but only because I fought for it. We'll still have to take a mortgage out.

And people resent that I got that. The guys at work tell my husband, Louis, that they're buying our house for us with their tax money. People don't understand that their tax dollars aren't in that forty-two million dollars. The money is from the Abandoned Mine Reclamation Fund, which comes from taxes on coal companies. And with all that money coming into Centralia, I don't think we got enough for our house.

The government treats themselves well with that money, but not us. The only one that stuck his neck out for us was (State Representative) Bob Belfanti. (Senators) Heinz and Specter came and went, made some promises during an election year. The people in town now don't care—the Redevelopment Authority and the Department of Health. They're here because this is where the money is.

I didn't participate in the health survey. If there's anything wrong with me now, I don't want to know. I'd be so bitter. They're a little late coming around with it. Nobody wants to do the darn thing. The only way they can get people to participate is by telling them they could get moved up on the priority list to move out.

JOAN GIROLAMI.

Joan Girolami on her last day in Centralia.

IT'S HARD TO admit that you need help, someone to talk to. I felt like John at the counseling center could really see how frightened the people were. He came to one meeting where a fist fight almost broke out.

The group sessions down there made a lot of things surface for me. I had to admit that I was carrying a lot of hate around in my heart. We didn't start the fire, but we got blamed for it. The hardest thing about counseling was admitting that we just had to quit.

I don't think I'd ever get involved in a citizens' group ever again unless there was a total commitment from people to help solve the problem. If you don't have that from people and you're on the front line, it's gonna wear you down and you're just gonna have so much hatred. There's no sense in it. You're wasting your time and your health fighting a problem that people don't care about solving. People have to be more aware of this stuff. They'll dump on their own property and then bury it with a bulldozer, and then they wonder why their water is bad.

You know, they say small towns are so nice. Put a tragedy in a small town, you'll find out how nice it is. Put a disaster there, and it's not so nice anymore.

JOAN GIROLAMI.

Irene (on bed) and Colleen Russen visit with Clara Gallagher shortly before her move from Centralia.

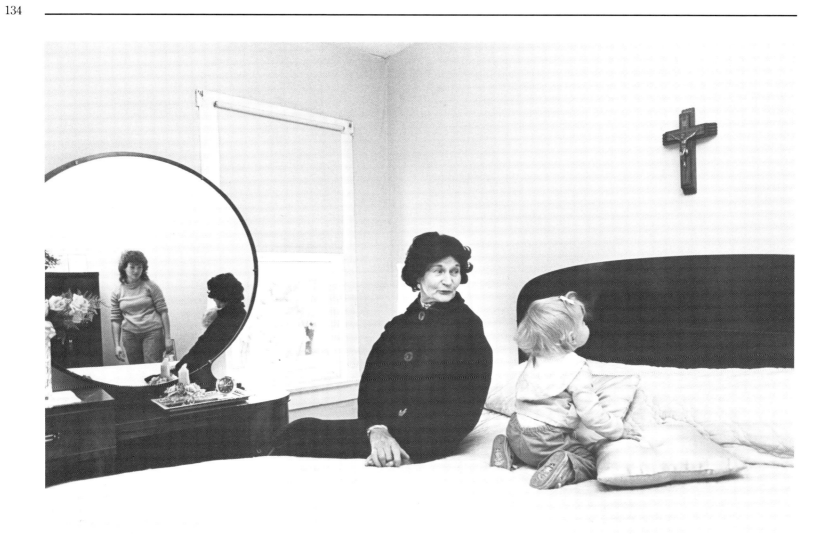

I WANTED TO stay here until I died. But it won't happen that way. And now I know I have to go. I hope I'm just as happy where I go as I was here. I will want to be buried back here. I have a lot up there, a place beside my husband. I don't want to go into a strange cemetery, so I think they'll bring me back.

That's what I want. To come back and be buried beside my husband. Coming all the way home again.

CLARA GALLAGHER.
Gallagher moved in with her daughter, Winnie, in Fairfax, Virginia, and died shortly thereafter.

Clara Gallagher, moving day.

I'VE LIVED HERE for forty-six years. When we moved into this house, it was very poorly built up. There was nothing in it. We remodeled it, put electric heat in, bathrooms, new sinks, fixed walls, windows, and doors. We tried to make it as modern as we could. The first thing we did was put the bathroom in about forty-two years ago. Before that we had a portable bathtub in the basement. It was rubber and folded up. You had to fill it by hand.

Everybody else is leaving, so I don't want to stay here. They said it wasn't good to live here, and I didn't want to live alone anymore. It frightens you to think that someday you could be found dead in bed from the fumes. I think those people who say there's no fire in Centralia sure are wrong. So I think it's best to leave everything behind and start a new life.

I'll miss living so close to the church. In Virginia I'll have to travel to the church. It will be about two miles, so I won't be able to walk. I'll miss the cemetery, and visiting Thomas, going to his grave, like I always did, twice a day.

CLARA GALLAGHER.

Moving day—after forty-six years.

The first day of demolition, December 14, 1984.

CENTRALIA WAS A nice little town. . . .

CLARA GALLAGHER.
Gallagher lived next door to the Jurgills,
whose home was the first to be demolished in
the forty-two-million-dollar relocation project.

The Jurgill home, December 14, 1984.

I DON'T THINK THERE is a word in the English language that describes how we feel walking around and seeing these boarded-up houses. When the ones went down over here, it was winter and we closed our curtains as much as we could. But now it's going to happen all through town. No matter where you are, you won't be able to get away from it. They're going to go through, seeing their neighbors' homes, memories, as though the house was once alive and now it is being slowly killed. That's what they'll feel when those houses start coming down. You're going to see it on every corner, every street. The part that gets me—it's all unnecessary. Absolutely unnecessary.

HELEN WOMER.

To SAY YOU WERE born here is one thing. To stay because you were born and raised here is one thing. But to say that you died here. . .

TODD DOMBOSKI.

Epilogue

I CANNOT RECALL the first time that I heard about the mine fire in Centralia. Surreal, ghostly images of smoke pouring from the ground have been in the back of my mind for as long as I can remember. My interest peaked one day in May 1983 when I came upon a series of detour signs directing the traffic of the curious around Centralia.

All I could imagine were visions of some hellish horror. I had heard the story of Todd Domboski, the teenager who had fallen into a smoky hole that had suddenly opened beneath his feet while he was walking in his grandmother's yard. The hole, later determined to be several hundred feet deep, contained a carbon monoxide count of eleven hundred parts per million, more than enough to cause brain damage and, in some instances, death. I had also heard of an entire block where children with documented upper respiratory problems lived in homes filled with the sound of gas monitors sniffing away in the dark.

Two weeks later, on a beautiful cloudless day, I ignored the detour signs on Route 61 and drove into the town. Except for the charred remains of a few uprooted trees, Centralia resembled any number of cozy, small coal towns in northeast Pennsylvania. People were congregated on porches and at the post office, swapping stories. There were no billowing clouds of smoke and certainly no flames leaping from the ground. The boreholes that dotted the landscape were quiet. It was not until much later that I learned the worst times in Centralia are the dreary, wet winter days. Then the smoke is thick, the stench sulfuric.

I spoke to several residents that day, and it became apparent that for many the greatest agony in Centralia was the fear of the unknown. The fact that the fire could not always be seen made the situation more difficult, not less. After all, how could the government, the media, and the general public identify with, and thereby remedy, a problem so difficult to pinpoint? The mine fire was truly an unseen enemy—shadowy and elusive like the carbon monoxide it gave off. Many in the town believed that if Centralia had been a natural disaster, such as a flood, assistance would have poured in.

But Centralia was a disaster unlike any other, a disaster with no bodies. No one seems quite sure how to deal with that fact. The duration of the fire has given it a horrible uniqueness in disaster lore. Never before has a population been exposed to such an unrelenting, insidious, yet unseen enemy. People have been born, married, and had children of their own—with the fire as a constant backdrop. Life in Centralia for a generation has been life with the mine fire: baseball games played by the steam vents; bicycles ridden around smoking boreholes; and every morning Joe, the caretaker at St. Ignatius, ringing the bell to summon the parishioners to church, calling them up the hill, past those boreholes and vents, to worship near where the fumes are at their worst.

Coping with the fire has been, and will continue to be, a complex, protracted process. In Centralia, chronic anxiety has led to a whole catalogue of ills—some of which may never heal. Some families have come out strengthened; many have been irrevocably torn apart. The town was fractured psychologically just as the ground would have been had a sudden subsidence split it in half, leaving a rumbling, smoking pit in the middle. Residents lost their sense that Centralia was a safe, benevolent world.

In Centralia, at this point, it is still hard to determine whether the mine fire, or individuals' perceptions of it, produced the greater health hazard. A health study conducted by the Hershey Medical Center showed that because of the fire and its related stress factors, Centralians suffered from a greater incidence of respiratory disease, hypertension, depression, and anxiety than residents of a similar town several miles away. As a local doctor put it, "I have a patient from Centralia with really bad nerves. He'd come in so many times, all worked up, all kinds of symptoms—indigestion, di-

arrhea, abdominal cramps, not sleeping at night. The patient said it wasn't as much the fire as getting his house sold and getting another place to live. But maybe the fire was the most convenient thing for him to worry about. There are so many different forms of stress—most people have some form or another. And with all the elderly people and chronic lung disease in this general area, it's hard to separate Centralia. I'd say only a few of my patients from Centralia, and there must be upwards of sixty, truly showed ill effects from the fire."

Health studies of areas like Centralia can prove invaluable, especially if correlated on a national level. Currently, many sources conservatively estimate that two hundred fifty mine fires and more than fifty thousand toxic waste dumps are scattered across the country. Centralians had gone to the government for many years, pleading for a health survey. Yet, as a Department of Health official told me, it was not even until 1982 that his office became staffed to do research of this kind.

Unlike Love Canal, where birth defects related to the toxic wastes were immediately apparent, the existence of chronic illnesses in Centralia will be proved or disproved only with the passage of time. Immediate health hazards come from potential exposure to a number of gases—carbon dioxide, carbon monoxide, sulfur, and methane. The short-term effects of that exposure could include headaches, dizziness, impaired motor coordination, convulsions, and respiratory failure. Indeed, mothers were told not to let children sniff the woodwork because gases could be particularly prevalent there.

Chronic exposure to gases emitted from the fire, coupled with oxygen deficiency and the possible presence of radon, could produce any number of illnesses. Additionally, these effects are exacerbated by several factors including old age and lung disease, problems that afflict a disproportionate number of town residents.

In its first ten years of funding projects for crisis counseling, the National Institute of Mental Health has given all thirty-three of its grants to short-term, mostly natural disasters. On a Federal Emergency Management Agency list of fifty-one frequently repeated disasters, twenty-one are instances of technology run amok.

In that respect, Centralia seems to take its place alongside Times Beach, Three Mile Island, and Love Canal as a testament to those instances in which human technological creations have gone mad. As Pennsylvania's Secretary of the Department of Environmental Resources Nicholas DeBenedictis has said, "The federal government moved swiftly when toxic contaminants were found at Love Canal and Times Beach, and certainly Centralia is no less a disaster and no less an emergency." The similarities, sadly, led a former Times Beach resident to write an anguished open letter to Centralians, advising them to take flower cuttings from their gardens with them to their new homes to ease the transition, a luxury she was not afforded because of the fear of contamination from dioxin. In Times Beach, she said, nature is now taking back the land. One wonders what is left to reclaim.

THE CHINESE WRITE the word "crisis" with two characters—one that means danger and the other opportunity. Centralia seems to demonstrate that in textbook fashion. Many people, through the support of their family, their faith, and in some instances counseling, were able to emerge strengthened from their involvement in the mine fire problem and in so doing turned a perilous situation into an opportunity for achievement and growth. People were forced to challenge their destiny, be resourceful and determined. In so doing, they exhibited an almost unyielding spirit despite repeated setbacks. It must be remembered, after all, that Centralians were deprived of an opportunity to make an informed decision about their future. At no time were they given the most important of all information—what, if anything, would be done to put out the fire.

Sadly, the information gathered from new mining maps indicates that the fire has spread more quickly than previously expected. Because nothing, as of this writing, has yet been undertaken to slow the fire's spread, Mt. Carmel, the town that many Centralians moved to, is now thought to be in much greater danger of being affected. Ironically, the west end of Mt. Carmel, where the fire will hit first if it spreads, is where many Centralians built their new homes.

IN THE MIDDLE OF June 1983, I moved into a home at the top of Centralia's impact zone. The house came not only equipped with a gas monitor but filled with memories of Catharene and Leon Jurgill, a young couple who had fled Centralia because their two daughters seemed chronically ill.

It was my desire to record, in words and photographs, the struggles of people who possessed more courage than I could fathom. I believed then, and even more so now, that the residents of Centralia represent us all. History has shown that it is not whether a disaster will strike a town, but when. If it is not a mine fire, it is living in the shadow of Three Mile Island. Or in a community with a tainted water supply. Or the ghastly horror of Bhopal.

The first time that I heard a gas monitor go off will stay with me for a very long time. I was sitting at the kitchen table in the Gasperetti household while the state inspectors from the Department of Environmental Resources moved around the house taking gas readings. The Gasperettis, like many families in Centralia, had somehow adapted to the continual presence of state and local officials testing, poking, and prodding. Mary Gasperetti did not even flinch when a shriek from the monitor split the room. It was, she sighed, a routine testing procedure.

Another vivid and chilling memory of Centralia is an image I saw as I left the house to photograph a Centralia sunrise. I crossed the street, rounded a corner, and headed to the scarred tract of land where many believe the fire started. In astonishing symmetry, the five wire-enmeshed vents were spitting black smoke straight up into the air, an eerie purple blue, in absolutely perfect, rigid, fifteen-foot plumes. It was one of the most alien things I have ever seen.

Now, when it snows, there is not a single sign that the Jurgill home, where their children were born and where I stayed for six months, ever existed. The people that lived in the block of four attached homes are scattered across Pennsylvania, Virginia, and California. Their homes took less than forty-five minutes to bulldoze. Instead of wrapping around the houses at the top of the hill, the smoke that floats from Route 61 now seems content to just drift eerily down Locust Avenue.

RENÉE JACOBS
January 1986